Scriptural Commands for Modern Times Living God's Word Today
Volume 2

Joshua Rhoades

Published by Joshua Paul Rhoades, 2024.

SCRIPTURAL COMMANDS FOR MODERN TIMES LIVING GOD'S WORD TODAY VOLUME 2

First edition. September 5, 2024.

ISBN: 979-8227263605

Written by Joshua Rhoades.

Also by Joshua Rhoades

Courage Under Fire: David's Stand On The Battlefield
Jonah's Journey: Voices Of Redemption And Lessons In Obedience
The Furnace Of Faith: 12 Principles From The Heat Of Faith
Whispers of Hope: Inspiring Stories of Men's Prayers In Scripture
Frontier Legends: The Oregon Dream
Elijah: A Beacon Of Boldness
HOOK, LINE & SAVIOUR - Faith Reflections from Fishing
Driven By Faith: Motor Racing Inspired Christian Life
30 Day Devotional - Bold and Strong- Coffee Devotions for a
Courageous Christian Walk
Authentic Christianity: The Heart of Old Time Religion
Consider The Ant - God's Tiny Preachers
Flee Fornication: The Plea For Purity
Renewed Hope- How to Find Encouragement in God
Sounding The Call - The Voice of Conviction
The Altar - Where Heaven Meets Earth
The Bible's Battlefields- Timeless Lessons from Ancient Wars
The Sacred Art of Silence - How Silence Speaks in Scripture
Under Fire- The Sanctity of the Traditional Biblical Home
Who Is on the Lord's Side? A Call to Righteousness
What Is Truth? - From Skepticism to Submission
First and Goal- Faith and Football Fundamentals
From Dugout to Devotion- Spiritual Lessons from Baseball
Par for the Course- Faith and Fairways
The Believer's Pace- Tools for Running Life's Marathon

Introduction

In today's world, where uncertainty and confusion seem to be the norm, the Bible offers a steady source of guidance and truth that is just as relevant now as it was thousands of years ago. "Scriptural Commands for Modern Times- Living God's Word Today Volume 2" continues the journey we began in the first volume, diving deeper into the commands of Scripture that are designed to help us navigate the complexities of life. This book is here to show that the Bible's teachings are not just old words on a page but living instructions that can help us face the challenges of today with wisdom and confidence. Throughout these pages, you'll find practical insights on how to apply God's commands to real-life situations, whether you're dealing with relationships, making tough decisions, or trying to live with integrity in a world that often seems to reward the opposite. Each chapter is a reminder that God's Word is not just about what we should avoid but about the kind of life we are called to live—a life full of purpose, peace, and the deep satisfaction that comes from following God's path. As you read through this book, you'll discover how these ancient commands speak directly to the issues we face in our modern lives, offering clear and practical guidance for how to live in a way that honors God and brings out the best in us. The commands we explore are not just rules to follow but are invitations to experience life the way God intended—full of love, joy, and meaning. By the end of this volume, you'll see how these commands can shape your thoughts, guide your actions, and influence every part of your life, helping you to grow closer to God and become the person He created you to be. So, as you turn these pages, be ready to be challenged, inspired, and equipped to live out God's Word in a world that needs His truth more than ever. This book is not just a continuation but a deeper dive into the life-changing power of

Scripture, and it's an invitation to let God's commands transform your life from the inside out.

Chapter 1 – Determination - "Be ye ready"

Matthew 24:44 - "Therefore be ye also ready: for in such an hour as ye think not the Son of man cometh."

This verse emphasizes diligence, urging believers to always be prepared for the return of Jesus Christ. To be ready means to live with a sense of constant preparedness and vigilance, ensuring that our lives reflect our faith and that we are always aligned with God's will. Diligence in this context refers to the careful and persistent effort to maintain a state of readiness, both spiritually and morally, in anticipation of Christ's return. This command encourages us to be proactive in our faith, to stay alert, and to live in a way that honors God at all times.

Being ready involves maintaining a strong and active relationship with God. This means regularly spending time in prayer, reading the Bible, and seeking God's guidance in our daily lives. By staying connected to God, we can remain sensitive to His leading and be more attuned to His purposes for us. This ongoing relationship helps to strengthen our faith and keep us focused on what truly matters.

Diligence requires us to be mindful of our actions and decisions, ensuring that they align with God's teachings. It means making choices that reflect our commitment to living a life of righteousness and integrity. This involves avoiding behaviors and attitudes that lead us away from God and instead, embracing those that draw us closer to Him. By being diligent in our actions, we demonstrate our readiness to follow God's will and to live according to His standards.

To be ready, we must also be watchful and alert to the signs of the times. This involves being aware of the spiritual and moral climate around us and recognizing the indicators of Christ's imminent return. By staying informed and discerning, we can better understand the urgency of our readiness and be more motivated to live faithfully. This vigilance helps us to avoid complacency and to remain focused on our spiritual growth and preparedness.

Diligence in being ready also involves being prepared to share our faith with others. This means being able to clearly and confidently communicate the message of the gospel and to answer questions about our beliefs. By being prepared to share our faith, we can be effective witnesses for Christ and help others to understand the importance of being ready for His return. This readiness to share the gospel reflects our commitment to fulfilling the Great Commission and to spreading the message of salvation.

Being ready also means being faithful in our responsibilities and duties. This involves diligently fulfilling the roles and tasks that God has entrusted to us, whether in our families, workplaces, or communities. By being faithful and responsible in our actions, we demonstrate our readiness to serve God and to be used by Him for His purposes. This diligence in our responsibilities helps to build a strong testimony of faithfulness and reliability.

Diligence requires us to be proactive in addressing areas of weakness and sin in our lives. This means regularly examining our hearts and actions, seeking God's forgiveness, and making efforts to grow and improve. By being diligent in our personal growth and repentance, we can stay on the path of righteousness and be more prepared for Christ's return. This ongoing process of self-examination and growth helps us to maintain a state of readiness and to live in a way that honors God.

To be ready, we must also cultivate a spirit of generosity and service. This involves using our time, talents, and resources to help others and to advance God's kingdom. By being generous and service-oriented, we demonstrate our readiness to be the hands and feet of Christ in the world. This spirit of service reflects our commitment to living out our faith in practical and impactful ways.

Diligence in being ready also involves building strong and supportive relationships with other believers. This means being an active part of a faith community, where we can encourage and support one another in our spiritual journeys. By being connected to other believers, we can receive the accountability and encouragement we need to stay ready and to grow in our faith. These relationships help to strengthen our resolve and to keep us focused on our readiness for Christ's return.

Being ready means living with a sense of urgency and purpose. It involves recognizing that our time on earth is limited and that we must make the most of every opportunity to live for God. This urgency helps to motivate us to be diligent in our faith and to avoid distractions and complacency. By living with purpose, we can ensure that our lives reflect our commitment to God and our readiness for His return.

Diligence in being ready also involves being hopeful and expectant. It means looking forward to Christ's return with anticipation and joy, knowing that His coming will bring fulfillment and restoration. This hope helps to sustain us through challenges and difficulties, giving us the strength and motivation to remain faithful. By maintaining a hopeful and expectant attitude, we can stay focused on the promise of Christ's return and be more diligent in our readiness.

To be ready, we must also be patient and persevering. This involves remaining steadfast in our faith, even when we face trials and uncertainties. By being patient and persevering, we demonstrate our trust in God's timing and our commitment to staying faithful, no matter what. This perseverance helps to build our character and to prepare us for Christ's return.

Diligence in being ready also means being open to the leading of the Holy Spirit. This involves being sensitive to the Spirit's guidance and willing to follow His direction. By being open to the Holy Spirit, we can be more effective in our readiness and more attuned to God's will. This openness helps to ensure that we are living in alignment with God's purposes and ready for Christ's return.

Being ready requires us to be disciplined in our spiritual practices. This means making regular time for prayer, Bible study, worship, and fellowship. By being disciplined in these practices, we can stay connected to God and maintain our readiness. This discipline helps to build a strong spiritual foundation and to keep us focused on our faith.

Diligence in being ready also involves being joyful and grateful. It means recognizing the blessings and grace that God has given us and responding with gratitude and joy. By being joyful and grateful, we can maintain a positive and hopeful attitude, even in the face of challenges. This joy and gratitude help to sustain us in our readiness and to reflect the light of Christ to others.

To be ready, we must also be mindful of our thoughts and attitudes. This involves being aware of negative or harmful thoughts and replacing them with thoughts that are true, noble, right, pure, lovely, and admirable, as described in Philippians 4:8. By being mindful of our thoughts, we can ensure that our minds are aligned with God's will and ready for Christ's return.

Diligence in being ready also means being committed to learning and growing. This involves being open to new insights and teachings, seeking to deepen our understanding of God's Word and His will for our lives. By being committed to learning and growing, we can stay ready and prepared for whatever God has in store for us. This commitment helps to keep our faith dynamic and alive.

Being ready means being adaptable and flexible. It involves being willing to adjust our plans and expectations to align with God's purposes. By being adaptable and flexible, we can stay open to the opportunities and challenges that come our way and remain ready for Christ's return. This flexibility helps to ensure that we are always in alignment with God's will.

Diligence in being ready also involves being reflective and contemplative. This means taking time to reflect on our lives, our faith, and our relationship with God. By being reflective and contemplative, we can gain deeper insights and understanding, helping us to stay ready and aligned with God's will. This reflection helps to build a strong spiritual foundation and to keep us focused on our readiness for Christ's return.

In conclusion, "Be ye ready" is a powerful command that emphasizes diligence. Matthew 24:44 urges believers to always be prepared for the return of Jesus Christ, living with a sense of constant preparedness and vigilance. To be ready means to live with careful and persistent effort, maintaining a state of readiness both spiritually and morally. Diligence involves maintaining a strong relationship with God, being mindful of our actions, staying watchful and alert, being prepared to share our faith, and being faithful in our responsibilities. It requires addressing areas of weakness and sin, cultivating a spirit of generosity and service, building strong relationships with other believers, living with urgency and purpose, being hopeful and expectant, and being patient and persevering. Diligence also means being open to the Holy Spirit, disciplined in our spiritual practices, joyful and grateful, mindful of our thoughts, committed to learning and growing, adaptable and flexible, and reflective and contemplative. This command is especially relevant in today's world, challenging us to live with purpose and readiness for Christ's return. By embracing this command, we can ensure that our lives reflect our faith and readiness, contributing to a culture of preparedness and diligence. In conclusion, "Be ye ready" is a command that calls for diligence, encouraging us to live in a way that honors God and demonstrates our readiness for Christ's return.

Chapter 2 – Delegation - "Cast thy burden upon the LORD"

Psalm 55:22 - "Cast thy burden upon the LORD, and he shall sustain thee: he shall never suffer the righteous to be moved."

This verse emphasizes delegation, urging believers to entrust their worries, cares, and responsibilities to God. To cast your burden upon the LORD means to transfer the weight of your problems and stresses onto Him, trusting that He will take care of you and support you. Delegation in this context refers to the act of handing over our anxieties and concerns to God, recognizing that He is more than capable of handling them. This command encourages us to let go of our burdens and rely on God's strength and provision, knowing that He cares for us and will sustain us through every challenge.

Casting our burdens upon the LORD begins with an attitude of trust and faith. It involves believing that God is willing and able to help us with our problems. This trust is built through a relationship with God, developed by spending time in prayer, reading the Bible, and reflecting on His faithfulness in our lives. By cultivating this trust, we can confidently bring our burdens to God, knowing that He is ready to take them from us and provide the support we need.

Delegation of our burdens requires us to acknowledge our limitations and recognize that we cannot handle everything on our own. It means admitting that we need God's help and being willing to rely on His strength instead of our own. This humility allows us to let go of the need to control every aspect of our lives and to surrender our problems to God. By doing so, we free ourselves from the weight of our burdens and open ourselves to God's sustaining power.

To cast our burdens upon the LORD, we must be intentional about bringing our concerns to Him in prayer. This involves regularly communicating with God, sharing our worries, fears, and challenges, and asking for His guidance and support. By making prayer a regular part of our lives, we create a habit of turning to God first when we are faced with difficulties. This practice helps us to develop a deeper sense of reliance on God and to experience His peace and comfort in the midst of our struggles.

Delegation also involves letting go of the things that weigh us down emotionally and mentally. This means releasing our anxieties, fears, and stressors to God, trusting that He will take care of them. It requires a conscious effort to stop dwelling on our problems and to focus instead on God's promises and faithfulness. By shifting our focus from our burdens to God's goodness, we can experience a sense of relief and freedom.

Casting our burdens upon the LORD means trusting in His timing and plan. It involves believing that God knows what is best for us and that He is working all things for our good. This trust allows us to let go of our worries about the future and to rest in the assurance that God is in control. By trusting in God's plan, we can experience peace and confidence, even when we do not understand how everything will work out.

Delegation requires us to be patient and to wait on God's timing. It means recognizing that God's ways are higher than our ways and that His timing is perfect. This patience helps us to remain steadfast and hopeful, even when we do not see immediate answers to our prayers. By waiting on God, we demonstrate our trust in His wisdom and His ability to provide for us.

To cast our burdens upon the LORD, we must also be willing to let go of our pride and self-reliance. It means acknowledging that we need God's help and being open to receiving His grace and support. This humility allows us to experience the fullness of God's sustaining power and to grow in our dependence on Him. By letting go of our pride, we can embrace the help that God offers and find strength in His provision.

Delegation involves being open to the ways that God may choose to support and sustain us. This can include seeking help from others, being willing to accept advice and assistance, and recognizing the resources that God has placed in our lives. By being open to these avenues of support, we can experience God's care in practical and tangible ways. This openness helps us to see God's hand at work in our lives and to appreciate the many ways He provides for us.

Casting our burdens upon the LORD also means being proactive in managing our stress and responsibilities. This involves taking practical steps to address our problems, such as organizing our tasks, setting priorities, and seeking solutions. By being diligent and responsible, we demonstrate our commitment to doing our part while trusting God to handle what is beyond our control. This balance of action and trust allows us to effectively manage our burdens and to experience God's sustaining power.

Delegation requires us to maintain a positive and hopeful attitude. It means focusing on God's promises and His faithfulness rather than on our problems and challenges. By keeping our minds fixed on God's goodness, we can experience peace and joy, even in difficult circumstances. This positive outlook helps us to stay encouraged and to trust in God's ability to sustain us.

To cast our burdens upon the LORD, we must also be willing to forgive ourselves and others. This involves letting go of past hurts, mistakes, and regrets, and trusting in God's forgiveness and grace. By forgiving ourselves and others, we release the emotional burdens that can weigh us down and prevent us from experiencing God's peace. This forgiveness allows us to move forward with a sense of freedom and hope.

Delegation involves being mindful of our physical and emotional well-being. It means taking care of our bodies and minds by getting enough rest, eating well, and seeking support when needed. By prioritizing our health, we can better manage our stress and responsibilities and be more open to receiving God's sustaining power. This mindfulness helps us to stay balanced and resilient in the face of challenges.

Casting our burdens upon the LORD means being grateful for the ways that God has already sustained us. It involves recognizing the many blessings and provisions that God has given us and expressing our gratitude. This gratitude helps to shift our focus from our problems to God's faithfulness and goodness. By cultivating a thankful heart, we can experience a greater sense of peace and contentment.

Delegation requires us to trust in God's provision and to believe that He will meet our needs. This means having faith that God will provide for us in ways that we may not expect or understand. By trusting in God's provision, we can let go of our worries and anxieties and rest in the assurance that He will take care of us. This trust allows us to experience God's sustaining power and to find peace in His care.

To cast our burdens upon the LORD, we must also be willing to surrender our plans and desires to God. This means being open to His will and being willing to let go of our own agendas. By surrendering our plans to God, we demonstrate our trust in His wisdom and His ability to guide us. This surrender allows us to experience the freedom and peace that come from being aligned with God's will.

Delegation involves being patient with ourselves and with God's timing. It means recognizing that change and solutions may take time and that we need to be patient and persistent. This patience allows us to stay hopeful and to trust in God's ability to sustain us through every challenge. By being patient, we can experience the peace and confidence that come from trusting in God's timing.

Casting our burdens upon the LORD means being open to the ways that God may choose to sustain us. This can include seeking help from others, being willing to accept advice and assistance, and recognizing the resources that God has placed in our lives. By being open to these avenues of support, we can experience God's care in practical and tangible ways. This openness helps us to see God's hand at work in our lives and to appreciate the many ways He provides for us.

Delegation requires us to maintain a positive and hopeful attitude. It means focusing on God's promises and His faithfulness rather than on our problems and challenges. By keeping our minds fixed on God's goodness, we can experience peace and joy, even in difficult circumstances. This positive outlook helps us to stay encouraged and to trust in God's ability to sustain us.

To cast our burdens upon the LORD, we must also be willing to forgive ourselves and others. This involves letting go of past hurts, mistakes, and regrets, and trusting in God's forgiveness and grace. By forgiving ourselves and others, we release the emotional burdens that can weigh us down and prevent us from experiencing God's peace. This forgiveness allows us to move forward with a sense of freedom and hope.

Delegation involves being mindful of our physical and emotional well-being. It means taking care of our bodies and minds by getting enough rest, eating well, and seeking support when needed. By prioritizing our health, we can better manage our stress and responsibilities and be more open to receiving God's sustaining power. This mindfulness helps us to stay balanced and resilient in the face of challenges.

Casting our burdens upon the LORD means being grateful for the ways that God has already sustained us. It involves recognizing the many blessings and provisions that God has given us and expressing our gratitude. This gratitude helps to shift our focus from our problems to God's faithfulness and goodness. By cultivating a thankful heart, we can experience a greater sense of peace and contentment.

Delegation requires us to trust in God's provision and to believe that He will meet our needs. This means having faith that God will provide for us in ways that we may not expect or understand. By trusting in God's provision, we can let go of our worries and anxieties and rest in the assurance that He will take care of us. This trust allows us to experience God's sustaining power and to find peace in His care.

To cast our burdens upon the LORD, we must also be willing to surrender our plans and desires to God. This means being open to His will and being willing to let go of our own agendas. By surrendering our plans to God, we demonstrate our trust in His wisdom and His ability to guide us. This surrender allows us to experience the freedom and peace that come from being aligned with God's will.

Delegation involves being patient with ourselves and with God's timing. It means recognizing that

change and solutions may take time and that we need to be patient and persistent. This patience allows us to stay hopeful and to trust in God's ability to sustain us through every challenge. By being patient, we can experience the peace and confidence that come from trusting in God's timing.

Casting our burdens upon the LORD means being open to the ways that God may choose to sustain us. This can include seeking help from others, being willing to accept advice and assistance, and recognizing the resources that God has placed in our lives. By being open to these avenues of support, we can experience God's care in practical and tangible ways. This openness helps us to see God's hand at work in our lives and to appreciate the many ways He provides for us.

Delegation requires us to maintain a positive and hopeful attitude. It means focusing on God's promises and His faithfulness rather than on our problems and challenges. By keeping our minds fixed on God's goodness, we can experience peace and joy, even in difficult circumstances. This positive outlook helps us to stay encouraged and to trust in God's ability to sustain us.

To cast our burdens upon the LORD, we must also be willing to forgive ourselves and others. This involves letting go of past hurts, mistakes, and regrets, and trusting in God's forgiveness and grace. By forgiving ourselves and others, we release the emotional burdens that can weigh us down and prevent us from experiencing God's peace. This forgiveness allows us to move forward with a sense of freedom and hope.

Delegation involves being mindful of our physical and emotional well-being. It means taking care of our bodies and minds by getting enough rest, eating well, and seeking support when needed. By prioritizing our health, we can better manage our stress and responsibilities and be more open to receiving God's sustaining power. This mindfulness helps us to stay balanced and resilient in the face of challenges.

Casting our burdens upon the LORD means being grateful for the ways that God has already sustained us. It involves recognizing the many blessings and provisions that God has given us and expressing our gratitude. This gratitude helps to shift our focus from our problems to God's faithfulness and goodness. By cultivating a thankful heart, we can experience a greater sense of peace and contentment.

Delegation requires us to trust in God's provision and to believe that He will meet our needs. This means having faith that God will provide for us in ways that we may not expect or understand. By trusting in God's provision, we can let go of our worries and anxieties and rest in the assurance that He will take care of us. This trust allows us to experience God's sustaining power and to find peace in His care.

To cast our burdens upon the LORD, we must also be willing to surrender our plans and desires to God. This means being open to His will and being willing to let go of our own agendas. By surrendering our plans to God, we demonstrate our trust in His wisdom and His ability to guide us. This surrender allows us to experience the freedom and peace that come from being aligned with God's will.

Delegation involves being patient with ourselves and with God's timing. It means recognizing that change and solutions may take time and that we need to be patient and persistent. This patience allows us to stay hopeful and to trust in God's ability to sustain us through every challenge. By being patient, we can experience the peace and confidence that come from trusting in God's timing.

In conclusion, "Cast thy burden upon the LORD" is a powerful command that emphasizes delegation. Psalm 55:22 urges believers to entrust their worries, cares, and responsibilities to God, recognizing that He is more than capable of handling them. To cast your burden upon the LORD means to transfer the weight of your problems and stresses onto Him, trusting that He will take care of you and support you. Delegation involves an attitude of trust and faith, acknowledging our limitations, and being intentional about bringing our concerns to God in prayer. It requires letting go of our anxieties and fears, trusting in God's timing and plan, and being willing to surrender our pride and self-reliance. Delegation also involves being open to the ways that God may choose to support and sustain us, maintaining a positive and hopeful attitude, and being proactive in managing our stress and responsibilities. It requires forgiveness, mindfulness of our physical and emotional well-being, and gratitude for God's sustaining power. By trusting in God's provision and surrendering our plans and desires to Him, we can experience the freedom and peace that come from being aligned with His will. This command challenges us to let go of our burdens and to rely on God's strength and provision, knowing that He cares for us and will sustain us through every challenge. By embracing this command, we can experience God's sustaining power and find peace and confidence in His care. In conclusion, "Cast thy burden upon the LORD" is a command that calls for delegation, encouraging us to entrust our burdens to God and to rely on His strength and provision, experiencing His peace and sustaining power in our lives.

Chapter 3 – Devotion - "Stand fast in the faith"

1 Corinthians 16:13 - "Watch ye, stand fast in the faith, quit you like men, be strong."

This verse emphasizes devotion, urging believers to remain steadfast and unwavering in their faith in God. To stand fast in the faith means to hold firmly to our beliefs, to be resolute in our commitment to God, and to persevere through challenges and temptations without wavering. Devotion in this context refers to a deep and unwavering commitment to God, characterized by loyalty, dedication, and faithfulness. This command encourages us to be vigilant, to maintain our faith with courage and strength, and to live out our beliefs consistently in every aspect of our lives.

Being devoted to standing fast in the faith involves having a strong foundation in God's Word. This means regularly reading and studying the Bible to understand God's teachings and to grow in our knowledge of Him. By grounding ourselves in Scripture, we can build a solid foundation for our faith that helps us to stand firm in the face of challenges and doubts. This deep knowledge of God's Word also equips us to defend our faith and to share it with others effectively.

Devotion requires us to be vigilant and watchful, as the verse begins with the command to "watch ye." This vigilance means being aware of the spiritual battles we face and recognizing the subtle ways in which our faith can be challenged. It involves staying alert to the influences and temptations that can lead us astray and being prepared to resist them. By being watchful, we can protect our faith and ensure that we remain steadfast in our commitment to God.

To stand fast in the faith, we must also be courageous and strong. The verse encourages us to "quit you like men, be strong," which means to act with bravery and resilience. This courage is essential when we face opposition or persecution for our beliefs. It involves standing up for what is right, even when it is difficult or unpopular. By demonstrating courage and strength, we show our devotion to God and our willingness to endure hardships for the sake of our faith.

Devotion also involves a continuous commitment to growing in our relationship with God. This means seeking Him daily through prayer, worship, and reflection. By cultivating a close and intimate relationship with God, we can draw strength and encouragement from His presence. This ongoing connection with God helps to sustain our faith and to deepen our devotion to Him.

Being devoted to standing fast in the faith requires us to be part of a supportive community of believers. Fellowship with other Christians provides encouragement, accountability, and support, helping us to remain steadfast in our faith. By being actively involved in a church or small group, we can build relationships with others who share our commitment to God and who can help us to stay strong in our faith. This sense of community reinforces our devotion and helps us to persevere through challenges.

To stand fast in the faith, we must also be committed to living out our beliefs in practical ways. This involves demonstrating our faith through our actions, such as showing love, kindness, and compassion to others. It means serving those in need, standing up for justice, and living with integrity and honesty. By living out our faith consistently, we demonstrate our devotion to God and provide a powerful witness to others.

Devotion requires us to be resilient and to persevere through difficulties. Faith is often tested through trials and hardships, and it is during these times that our commitment to God is most crucial. By remaining steadfast and trusting in God's faithfulness, we can overcome obstacles and grow stronger in our faith. This perseverance is a key aspect of standing fast in the faith and demonstrates our unwavering dedication to God.

Being devoted to standing fast in the faith also involves maintaining a hopeful and positive attitude. It means trusting in God's promises and believing that He is in control, even when circumstances are challenging. By focusing on God's goodness and faithfulness, we can find peace and encouragement in the midst of difficulties. This hopeful outlook helps us to remain steadfast and devoted, knowing that God is with us and that He will see us through.

Devotion requires us to be disciplined in our spiritual practices. This means making time for regular prayer, Bible study, worship, and reflection. By being disciplined in these practices, we can strengthen our faith and stay connected to God. This discipline helps to build a strong foundation for our devotion and enables us to stand firm in our beliefs.

To stand fast in the faith, we must also be willing to make sacrifices for the sake of our commitment to God. This can involve giving up certain comforts, pleasures, or even relationships that hinder our walk with God. By being willing to make these sacrifices, we demonstrate our devotion and our desire to prioritize our relationship with God above all else. This sacrificial mindset helps to keep our focus on God and to maintain our steadfastness in the faith.

Devotion involves being open to the guidance and leading of the Holy Spirit. It means being sensitive to the Spirit's prompting and willing to follow His direction. By being open to the Holy Spirit, we can receive the strength and wisdom we need to stand firm in our faith. This openness allows us to be responsive to God's will and to remain steadfast in our commitment to Him.

Being devoted to standing fast in the faith also involves continually seeking to grow and mature spiritually. This means being open to learning and growing in our understanding of God's Word and His will for our lives. By pursuing spiritual growth, we can deepen our faith and strengthen our commitment to God. This continuous growth helps to keep our faith dynamic and alive.

Devotion requires us to be patient and to trust in God's timing. It means recognizing that God's plans and purposes often unfold in ways that we do not expect or understand. By being patient and trusting in God's timing, we can remain steadfast in our faith, knowing that He is in control. This trust helps to sustain us through uncertainties and challenges, reinforcing our devotion to God.

To stand fast in the faith, we must also be committed to sharing our faith with others. This involves being willing to speak about our beliefs and to share the message of the gospel. By being bold in our witness, we demonstrate our devotion to God and our desire to see others come to know Him. This commitment to evangelism is an important aspect of standing fast in the faith and reflects our dedication to fulfilling God's mission.

Devotion involves being grateful for God's faithfulness and provision in our lives. It means recognizing the many ways that God has blessed and sustained us and expressing our gratitude. By cultivating a thankful heart, we can remain positive and hopeful, even in challenging times. This gratitude helps to reinforce our faith and to maintain our devotion to God.

Being devoted to standing fast in the faith requires us to be humble and to recognize our dependence on God. It means acknowledging that we need God's strength and guidance to remain steadfast. By being humble and dependent on God, we can draw on His resources and find the strength we need to persevere. This humility helps to keep our focus on God and to maintain our devotion to Him.

In conclusion, "Stand fast in the faith" is a powerful command that emphasizes devotion. 1 Corinthians 16:13 urges believers to remain steadfast and unwavering in their faith in God, holding firmly to their beliefs and persevering through challenges with courage and strength. Devotion involves a deep and unwavering commitment to God, characterized by loyalty, dedication, and faithfulness. It requires a strong foundation in God's Word, vigilance and watchfulness, courage and strength, continuous growth in our relationship with God, and being part of a supportive community of believers. Devotion also involves living out our beliefs in practical ways, demonstrating our faith through our actions, and being resilient and hopeful in the face of difficulties. It requires discipline in our spiritual practices, willingness to make sacrifices, openness to the Holy Spirit, patience and trust in God's timing, commitment to sharing our faith, gratitude for God's faithfulness, and humility and dependence on God. This command is especially relevant in today's world, challenging us to live with steadfastness and devotion to God. By embracing this command, we can ensure that our lives reflect our faith and devotion, contributing to a culture of faithfulness and perseverance. In conclusion, "Stand fast in the faith" is a command that calls for devotion, encouraging us to live in a way that honors God and demonstrates our unwavering commitment to Him.

Chapter 4 – Diplomacy - "Be ye reconciled to God"

2 Corinthians 5:20 - "Now then we are ambassadors for Christ, as though God did beseech you by us: we pray you in Christ's stead, be ye reconciled to God."

This verse emphasizes diplomacy, urging believers to restore their relationship with God through Jesus Christ. To be reconciled to God means to bridge the gap caused by sin, to mend our relationship with Him, and to embrace the peace and unity that come from being in right standing with Him. Diplomacy in this context refers to the act of negotiating and restoring a broken relationship, recognizing the need for reconciliation, and taking steps to achieve it. This command encourages us to accept God's offer of forgiveness and to live in harmony with Him, reflecting His love and grace in our lives.

Being reconciled to God begins with understanding the significance of our relationship with Him. Sin creates a separation between us and God, and reconciliation is the process of healing that divide. It involves acknowledging our sins, feeling genuine remorse, and seeking God's forgiveness through Jesus Christ. By recognizing our need for reconciliation, we take the first step towards restoring our relationship with God and experiencing His grace and mercy.

Diplomacy in reconciliation requires humility and a willingness to admit our faults. It means being honest with ourselves about our shortcomings and taking responsibility for our actions. This humility allows us to approach God with a contrite heart, ready to seek His forgiveness and to make amends. By being humble, we demonstrate our sincere desire to be reconciled to God and to restore the relationship that sin has damaged.

To be reconciled to God, we must also accept the gift of salvation offered through Jesus Christ. Jesus' sacrifice on the cross provides the means for our reconciliation with God, as He took the penalty for our sins upon Himself. By placing our faith in Jesus and accepting His sacrifice, we can receive God's forgiveness and be restored to a right relationship with Him. This acceptance is a crucial aspect of reconciliation, as it acknowledges the central role of Jesus in bridging the gap between us and God.

Diplomacy involves actively seeking to maintain a close and intimate relationship with God. This means regularly spending time in prayer, reading the Bible, and worshiping Him. By staying connected to God through these spiritual practices, we can deepen our relationship with Him and ensure that we remain in harmony with His will. This ongoing connection helps to prevent future breaches in our relationship and keeps us aligned with God's purposes for our lives.

Being reconciled to God also means living in a way that reflects His love and grace. This involves demonstrating the qualities of forgiveness, compassion, and kindness in our interactions with others. By living out these principles, we show that we have truly embraced God's forgiveness and are committed to living in accordance with His will. This reflection of God's character in our lives serves as a powerful testimony to others and helps to promote reconciliation in our relationships with them.

Diplomacy requires us to be peacemakers, both in our relationship with God and in our relationships with others. It means actively seeking to resolve conflicts, to promote understanding, and to foster harmony. By being peacemakers, we can help to create an environment where reconciliation is possible and where relationships can be restored. This commitment to peace and reconciliation is a key aspect of being ambassadors for Christ, as we seek to reflect His love and grace in all that we do.

To be reconciled to God, we must also be willing to forgive ourselves. This involves letting go of guilt and shame and accepting God's forgiveness and grace. By forgiving ourselves, we can experience the freedom and peace that come from being reconciled to God. This self-forgiveness is an important part of the healing process and helps us to move forward in our relationship with God with confidence and joy.

Diplomacy in reconciliation involves being patient and persistent. Reconciliation is often a process that takes time and effort, and it requires a commitment to working through challenges and obstacles. By being patient and persistent, we can persevere in our efforts to restore our relationship with God and to maintain that relationship over time. This persistence demonstrates our dedication to reconciliation and our desire to be in right standing with God.

Being reconciled to God also means being open to His guidance and direction. It involves being willing to listen to God's voice and to follow His leading in our lives. By being open to God's guidance, we can align our actions and decisions with His will and ensure that we are living in accordance with His purposes. This openness helps to maintain our reconciliation with God and to keep us on the path of righteousness.

Diplomacy requires us to be accountable in our relationship with God. This means being honest with ourselves and with God about our struggles and shortcomings and seeking His help to overcome them. By being accountable, we can stay on track in our relationship with God and avoid falling back into patterns of sin. This accountability helps to strengthen our commitment to reconciliation and to keep us focused on our relationship with God.

To be reconciled to God, we must also be willing to extend forgiveness to others. Just as God has forgiven us, we are called to forgive those who have wronged us. This forgiveness is a crucial aspect of reconciliation, as it allows us to release bitterness and resentment and to experience the peace and freedom that come from being in right relationships. By forgiving others, we demonstrate our commitment to living in accordance with God's will and to promoting reconciliation in all areas of our lives.

Diplomacy involves being proactive in seeking reconciliation. This means taking the initiative to address issues and conflicts and to work towards resolution. By being proactive, we can prevent small issues from becoming larger problems and can maintain healthy and harmonious relationships. This proactive approach helps to promote reconciliation and to ensure that our relationships are strong and healthy.

Being reconciled to God also means being grateful for His forgiveness and grace. It involves recognizing the incredible gift of salvation and expressing our gratitude through our actions and attitudes. By cultivating a thankful heart, we can remain focused on God's goodness and grace and stay motivated to live in accordance with His will. This gratitude helps to reinforce our commitment to reconciliation and to keep us aligned with God's purposes.

Diplomacy requires us to be compassionate and understanding. It means being empathetic to the struggles and challenges of others and being willing to offer support and encouragement. By being compassionate, we can create an environment where reconciliation is possible and where relationships can be healed. This compassion reflects the love of Christ and helps to promote reconciliation in our relationships.

To be reconciled to God, we must also be committed to personal growth and spiritual development. This involves continually seeking to grow in our understanding of God's Word and His will for our lives. By pursuing spiritual growth, we can deepen our relationship with God and strengthen our commitment to reconciliation. This continuous growth helps to keep our faith dynamic and alive and to ensure that we remain in right standing with God.

Diplomacy in reconciliation involves being adaptable and flexible. It means being willing to adjust our approaches and strategies to achieve reconciliation and to maintain healthy relationships. By being adaptable, we can respond effectively to different situations and challenges and can promote reconciliation in a variety of contexts. This flexibility helps to ensure that we are always working towards harmony and unity in our relationships.

Being reconciled to God also means being honest and transparent in our relationship with Him. It involves being open about our struggles and challenges and seeking God's help and guidance. By being honest with God, we can experience His grace and support and can maintain a healthy and authentic relationship with Him. This honesty helps to strengthen our commitment to reconciliation and to keep us aligned with God's will.

Diplomacy requires us to be hopeful and optimistic. It means believing that reconciliation is possible and that God is able to heal and restore our relationships. By maintaining a hopeful attitude, we can stay motivated and encouraged in our efforts to seek reconciliation. This hope helps to sustain us through challenges and to keep us focused on the goal of harmony and unity.

To be reconciled to God, we must also be committed to living out our faith in practical ways. This involves demonstrating our commitment to God through our actions, such as showing love, kindness, and compassion to others. By living out our faith, we demonstrate our commitment to reconciliation and to reflecting God's love in all that we do. This practical expression of our faith helps to promote reconciliation and to ensure that we are living in accordance with God's will.

Diplomacy involves being respectful and considerate in our interactions with others. It means treating others with dignity and respect, even when we disagree or face conflicts. By being respectful, we can create an environment where reconciliation is possible and where relationships can be healed. This respect reflects the love of Christ and helps to promote reconciliation in our relationships.

Being reconciled to God also means being committed to seeking justice and righteousness. It involves standing up for what is right and working towards creating a more just and equitable world. By seeking justice, we demonstrate our commitment to living in accordance with God's will and to promoting reconciliation in all areas of our lives. This commitment to justice helps to ensure that our relationships are strong and healthy.

Diplomacy requires us to be patient and persistent in our efforts to seek reconciliation. It means being willing to work through challenges and obstacles and to persevere in our commitment to reconciliation. By being patient and persistent, we can achieve reconciliation and maintain healthy relationships. This persistence demonstrates our dedication to reconciliation and our desire to be in right standing with God.

To be reconciled to God, we must also be willing to seek help and support when needed. This involves reaching out to others for guidance, encouragement, and accountability. By seeking help, we can stay on track in our relationship with God and can overcome challenges and obstacles. This support helps to strengthen our commitment to reconciliation and to keep us focused on our relationship with God.

Diplomacy involves being proactive in seeking opportunities to promote reconciliation. This means looking for ways to build bridges and to foster harmony in our relationships. By being proactive, we can create an environment where reconciliation is possible and where relationships can be healed. This proactive approach helps to

promote reconciliation and to ensure that our relationships are strong and healthy.

Being reconciled to God also means being committed to personal growth and spiritual development. This involves continually seeking to grow in our understanding of God's Word and His will for our lives. By pursuing spiritual growth, we can deepen our relationship with God and strengthen our commitment to reconciliation. This continuous growth helps to keep our faith dynamic and alive and to ensure that we remain in right standing with God.

Diplomacy in reconciliation involves being adaptable and flexible. It means being willing to adjust our approaches and strategies to achieve reconciliation and to maintain healthy relationships. By being adaptable, we can respond effectively to different situations and challenges and can promote reconciliation in a variety of contexts. This flexibility helps to ensure that we are always working towards harmony and unity in our relationships.

In conclusion, "Be ye reconciled to God" is a powerful command that emphasizes diplomacy. 2 Corinthians 5:20 urges believers to restore their relationship with God through Jesus Christ, recognizing the need for reconciliation and taking steps to achieve it. Diplomacy involves humility, acceptance of salvation, active maintenance of our relationship with God, living out His love and grace, being peacemakers, self-forgiveness, patience, and persistence. It requires being open to God's guidance, being accountable, extending forgiveness, being proactive, showing gratitude, demonstrating compassion, pursuing personal growth, being adaptable, and maintaining a hopeful and optimistic attitude. By embracing this command, we can ensure that our lives reflect our commitment to reconciliation with God, contributing to a culture of harmony and unity. In conclusion, "Be ye reconciled to God" is a command that calls for diplomacy, encouraging us to restore and maintain a right relationship with God and to reflect His love and grace in our lives.

Chapter 5 – Defense - "Put on the whole armour of God"

Ephesians 6:11 - "Put on the whole armour of God, that ye may be able to stand against the wiles of the devil."

This verse emphasizes defense, urging believers to protect themselves spiritually by equipping themselves with God's armor. To put on the whole armor of God means to prepare and arm ourselves with the spiritual tools and protections that God provides to withstand the challenges and temptations we face from the devil. Defense in this context refers to the proactive steps we take to safeguard our faith and remain steadfast in our commitment to God. This command encourages us to be vigilant, to use the resources God has given us, and to stand firm in our faith despite the trials we encounter.

Being defensively equipped begins with understanding what the armor of God entails. According to Ephesians 6:14-17, the armor includes the belt of truth, the breastplate of righteousness, the gospel of peace as shoes, the shield of faith, the helmet of salvation, and the sword of the Spirit, which is the Word of God. Each piece of this spiritual armor has a specific purpose and offers unique protection against the devil's schemes. By putting on this armor, we prepare ourselves to face spiritual battles with strength and confidence.

Defense requires us to embrace and live by the truth. The belt of truth represents the importance of honesty and integrity in our lives. By holding onto God's truth and rejecting lies and deceit, we build a solid foundation for our faith. This truth guides our actions and decisions, helping us to live in a way that honors God. By being truthful, we protect ourselves from the devil's attempts to deceive and mislead us.

The breastplate of righteousness symbolizes living a life of moral integrity and uprightness. By striving to live according to God's standards and maintaining a pure heart, we guard ourselves against the devil's attacks on our character and morality. This righteousness is not about being perfect but about seeking to align our lives with God's will and relying on His grace to overcome our shortcomings. By wearing the breastplate of righteousness, we protect our hearts and ensure that our actions reflect our faith.

The gospel of peace as shoes represents the readiness and stability that come from knowing and sharing the good news of Jesus Christ. By grounding ourselves in the gospel, we can stand firm and remain unshaken by the challenges we face. This peace helps us to navigate difficult situations with calmness and confidence, knowing that we are secure in God's love. By being prepared to share the gospel, we also spread God's peace to others, strengthening our own faith and encouraging those around us.

The shield of faith is crucial for protecting us from the devil's attacks, such as doubts, fears, and temptations. By holding up the shield of faith, we can extinguish these fiery darts and remain steadfast in our trust in God. Faith acts as a protective barrier, giving us the confidence to face challenges without being overwhelmed. By maintaining a strong and active faith, we shield ourselves from the negative influences that seek to undermine our relationship with God.

The helmet of salvation protects our minds, reminding us of our identity in Christ and the hope we have in Him. By focusing on our salvation and the promises of eternal life, we guard our thoughts against doubts and discouragement. This helmet helps us to stay positive and hopeful, even in the face of adversity. By remembering that we are saved and loved by God, we can face challenges with assurance and peace.

The sword of the Spirit, which is the Word of God, is our primary offensive weapon against the devil. By studying and knowing the Bible, we can use Scripture to counter the devil's lies and temptations. The Word of God is powerful and effective, providing guidance, strength, and encouragement. By wielding this sword, we can stand firm in our faith and overcome the challenges we face. This active engagement with God's Word strengthens our defense and equips us to stand against the devil's schemes.

Defense requires us to be vigilant and aware of the spiritual battles we face. It means recognizing that we are in a constant struggle against spiritual forces and being prepared to respond accordingly. By staying alert and watchful, we can identify the devil's tactics and take steps to protect ourselves. This vigilance helps us to stay grounded in our faith and to avoid being caught off guard by temptations or attacks.

Putting on the whole armor of God involves a daily commitment to spiritual readiness. It means starting each day with prayer, seeking God's guidance, and intentionally putting on each piece of the armor. By making this a daily practice, we ensure that we are always prepared to face whatever challenges come our way. This commitment to daily readiness strengthens our defense and helps us to live in a way that honors God.

Defense also requires us to rely on God's strength rather than our own. The armor of God is not something we can create or sustain on our own; it is a gift from God that we must actively put on and depend upon. By trusting in God's power and provision, we can face challenges with confidence and strength. This reliance on God helps us to recognize our dependence on Him and to seek His help in times of need.

Being defensively equipped means surrounding ourselves with a supportive community of believers. Fellowship with other Christians provides encouragement, accountability, and support in our spiritual battles. By being part of a faith community, we can share our struggles, receive prayer, and find strength in the collective faith of others. This sense of community reinforces our defense and helps us to stand firm in our faith.

Defense involves being proactive in addressing areas of weakness and vulnerability. By identifying the aspects of our lives where we are most susceptible to temptation or attack, we can take steps to strengthen our defenses. This might include seeking counsel, setting boundaries, or developing new habits that support our spiritual growth. By being proactive, we can fortify our defense and protect ourselves from the devil's schemes.

Putting on the whole armor of God also means being committed to spiritual growth and development. This involves continually seeking to deepen our understanding of God's Word, to grow in our relationship with Him, and to develop our spiritual disciplines. By pursuing spiritual growth, we can strengthen our defense and ensure that we are well-equipped to stand against the devil's attacks. This commitment to growth helps us to stay strong and resilient in our faith.

Defense requires us to be prayerful and to seek God's guidance and protection continually. Prayer is a vital part of putting on the armor of God, as it connects us to His power and provision. By praying for God's protection, wisdom, and strength, we can fortify our defense and remain steadfast in our faith. This reliance on prayer helps us to stay connected to God and to draw on His resources in times of need.

Being defensively equipped also involves maintaining a positive and hopeful attitude. By focusing on God's promises and His faithfulness, we can remain encouraged and motivated, even in the face of challenges. This positive outlook helps us to stay strong in our faith and to resist the devil's attempts to discourage us. By cultivating hope and positivity, we reinforce our defense and demonstrate our trust in God's provision.

Defense involves being disciplined in our spiritual practices. This means making regular time for prayer, Bible study, worship, and reflection. By being disciplined in these practices, we can strengthen our defense and stay connected to God. This discipline helps to build a strong spiritual foundation and to keep us focused on our faith.

Putting on the whole armor of God also means being adaptable and flexible. It involves being willing to adjust our strategies and approaches to suit different challenges and situations. By being adaptable, we can respond effectively to the devil's tactics and maintain our defense in a variety of contexts. This flexibility helps to ensure that we are always prepared and equipped to stand firm in our faith.

Defense requires us to be humble and to recognize our need for God's help. It means acknowledging that we cannot stand against the devil's attacks on our own and that we need God's strength and guidance. By being humble, we open ourselves to God's provision and support, which strengthens our defense. This humility helps us to stay reliant on God and to seek His help in times of need.

Being defensively equipped means being committed to living out our faith in practical ways. This involves demonstrating our commitment to God through our actions, such as showing love, kindness, and compassion to others. By living out our faith, we strengthen our defense and provide a powerful witness to others. This practical expression of our faith helps to promote God's kingdom and to protect us from the devil's schemes.

Defense involves being grateful for God's protection and provision in our lives. It means recognizing the many ways that God has safeguarded and sustained us and expressing our gratitude. By cultivating a thankful heart, we can remain focused on God's goodness and faithfulness. This gratitude helps to reinforce our defense and to maintain our trust in God's provision.

Putting on the whole armor of God means being committed to sharing our faith with others. By being willing to speak about our beliefs and to share the message of the gospel, we demonstrate our commitment to God's kingdom. This willingness to share our faith strengthens our defense and helps to spread God's love and truth. By being active in evangelism, we contribute to the growth of God's kingdom and protect ourselves from the devil's attacks.

In conclusion, "Put on the whole armour of God" is a powerful command that emphasizes defense. Ephesians 6:11 urges believers to protect themselves spiritually by equipping themselves with God's armor to withstand the challenges and temptations from the devil. Defense involves understanding and using each piece of God's armor—truth, righteousness, the gospel of peace, faith, salvation, and the Word of God. It requires vigilance, daily commitment, reliance on God's strength, and being part of a supportive community. Defense also involves being proactive, disciplined, prayerful, positive, adaptable, humble, and grateful. By embracing this command, we ensure that our lives reflect our commitment to God's protection and provision, contributing to a culture of spiritual readiness and resilience. In conclusion, "Put on the whole armour of God" is a command that calls for defense, encouraging us to protect ourselves spiritually and to stand firm in our faith against the devil's schemes.

Chapter 6 - Delight - "Delight thyself also in the LORD"

Psalm 37:4 - "Delight thyself also in the LORD; and he shall give thee the desires of thine heart."

This verse emphasizes delight, urging believers to find their greatest joy and satisfaction in God. To delight in the LORD means to take pleasure in knowing Him, to cherish His presence, and to find fulfillment in His love and guidance. Delight in this context refers to experiencing a deep, abiding joy and contentment that comes from a close relationship with God. This command encourages us to focus our hearts and minds on God, to seek our happiness in Him, and to trust that He will fulfill our deepest desires as we align our will with His.

Delighting in the LORD begins with cultivating a relationship with Him. This involves spending time in prayer, reading the Bible, and worshiping God. By making these practices a regular part of our lives, we can grow closer to God and develop a deeper understanding of His character and His love for us. This growing relationship helps to shift our focus from worldly pleasures to the lasting joy that comes from knowing and loving God.

To delight in the LORD, we must also trust in His goodness and faithfulness. It means believing that God has our best interests at heart and that He is working all things for our good. This trust allows us to find joy and contentment in God's plans and purposes for our lives, even when we do not fully understand them. By trusting in God's goodness, we can let go of anxiety and worry, and rest in the assurance that He is in control.

Delight involves being grateful for God's blessings and provisions. It means recognizing the many ways that God has blessed us and expressing our gratitude through praise and thanksgiving. By focusing on God's goodness and faithfulness, we can cultivate a heart of gratitude that enhances our joy and contentment in Him. This gratitude helps to keep our hearts aligned with God's will and to remind us of His constant presence and provision in our lives.

Delighting in the LORD also means finding joy in His Word. The Bible is a rich source of wisdom, encouragement, and inspiration, and by studying it, we can gain a deeper understanding of God's character and His will for our lives. By immersing ourselves in Scripture, we can find joy and satisfaction in the truths and promises it contains. This engagement with God's Word helps to deepen our relationship with Him and to strengthen our faith.

To delight in the LORD, we must also find joy in serving Him and others. This involves using our gifts and talents to serve God's purposes and to bless those around us. By serving others, we can experience the joy that comes from making a positive impact and from living out our faith in practical ways. This service helps to align our desires with God's will and to find fulfillment in contributing to His kingdom.

Delight requires us to focus on the eternal rather than the temporary. It means finding our joy in the things that have lasting value, such as our relationship with God, our spiritual growth, and our impact on others. By shifting our focus from temporary pleasures to eternal truths, we can experience a deeper and more lasting joy. This perspective helps to keep our hearts and minds centered on God and His purposes.

To delight in the LORD, we must also be willing to surrender our desires to Him. This means trusting that God's plans and purposes for our lives are better than our own and being willing to let go of our own agendas. By surrendering our desires to God, we can experience the joy and fulfillment that come from aligning our will with His. This surrender allows us to find true contentment in God's plans for our lives.

Delight involves being patient and waiting on God's timing. It means trusting that God knows the perfect time and way to fulfill our desires and being willing to wait for His timing. This patience helps us to remain hopeful and content, even when we do not see immediate answers to our prayers. By waiting on God, we can experience the joy of seeing His plans unfold in His perfect timing.

To delight in the LORD, we must also be open to the ways that God wants to work in and through us. This means being willing to step out in faith and to follow God's leading, even when it is challenging or uncomfortable. By being open to God's plans, we can experience the joy of being used by Him to make a difference in the world. This openness helps to deepen our relationship with God and to align our desires with His will.

Delight requires us to be content in all circumstances. It means finding joy and satisfaction in God, regardless of our external circumstances. By focusing on God's presence and His promises, we can experience a deep and abiding joy that is not dependent on our situation. This contentment helps to keep our hearts centered on God and to remind us of His constant care and provision.

To delight in the LORD, we must also prioritize our relationship with Him above all else. This means making time for God in our busy lives and putting Him first in our hearts and minds. By prioritizing our relationship with God, we can experience the joy and fulfillment that come from being close to Him. This prioritization helps to keep our hearts aligned with God's will and to remind us of the importance of our relationship with Him.

Delight involves being joyful in God's presence. It means finding pleasure in spending time with God, in worshiping Him, and in experiencing His love. By being joyful in God's presence, we can experience a deeper and more fulfilling relationship with Him. This joy helps to strengthen our faith and to keep our hearts centered on God.

To delight in the LORD, we must also be willing to seek Him with all our hearts. This means making a conscious effort to pursue God and to deepen our relationship with Him. By seeking God with all our hearts, we can experience the joy and fulfillment that come from knowing and loving Him. This pursuit helps to keep our hearts aligned with God's will and to remind us of the importance of our relationship with Him.

Delight requires us to find joy in the simple things. It means recognizing the beauty and goodness in the everyday moments and finding pleasure in God's creation. By finding joy in the simple things, we can experience a deeper and more lasting contentment. This recognition helps to keep our hearts centered on God and to remind us of His constant presence and provision.

To delight in the LORD, we must also be willing to trust Him with our future. This means believing that God has good plans for our lives and being willing to follow His leading. By trusting God with our future, we can experience the joy and peace that come from knowing that He is in control. This trust helps to keep our hearts aligned with God's will and to remind us of His constant care and provision.

Delight involves being thankful for God's presence in our lives. It means recognizing the many ways that God is with us and expressing our gratitude for His constant care and provision. By being thankful for God's presence, we can experience a deeper and more lasting joy. This gratitude helps to keep our hearts centered on God and to remind us of His constant presence and provision.

To delight in the LORD, we must also be willing to let go of our worries and fears. This means trusting that God is in control and that He will take care of us. By letting go of our worries and fears, we can experience the joy and peace that come from trusting in God's care. This trust helps to keep our hearts aligned with God's will and to remind us of His constant care and provision.

Delight requires us to focus on the positive aspects of our lives. It means recognizing the good things that God has given us and focusing on them rather than on our problems. By focusing on the positive aspects of our lives, we can experience a deeper and more lasting joy.

This focus helps to keep our hearts centered on God and to remind us of His constant presence and provision.

To delight in the LORD, we must also be willing to serve Him with joy. This means using our gifts and talents to serve God's purposes and to bless others. By serving God with joy, we can experience the fulfillment and satisfaction that come from living out our faith in practical ways. This service helps to keep our hearts aligned with God's will and to remind us of the importance of our relationship with Him.

Delight involves being hopeful and optimistic about the future. It means believing that God has good plans for our lives and being willing to trust Him with our future. By being hopeful and optimistic, we can experience the joy and peace that come from trusting in God's care. This hope helps to keep our hearts centered on God and to remind us of His constant presence and provision.

To delight in the LORD, we must also be willing to forgive ourselves and others. This means letting go of past hurts, mistakes, and regrets, and accepting God's forgiveness and grace. By forgiving ourselves and others, we can experience the joy and peace that come from being reconciled to God. This forgiveness helps to keep our hearts aligned with God's will and to remind us of His constant care and provision.

Delight requires us to be content with what we have. It means recognizing that God has given us everything we need and being satisfied with His provision. By being content with what we have, we can experience a deeper and more lasting joy. This contentment helps to keep our hearts centered on God and to remind us of His constant presence and provision.

To delight in the LORD, we must also be willing to trust Him with our desires. This means believing that God knows what is best for us and being willing to let go of our own agendas. By trusting God with our desires, we can experience the joy and fulfillment that come from aligning our will with His. This trust helps to keep our hearts aligned with God's will and to remind us of His constant care and provision.

Delight involves being joyful in God's promises. It means finding pleasure in the truths and assurances that God has given us and holding onto them in faith. By being joyful in God's promises, we can experience a deeper and more lasting contentment. This joy helps to keep our hearts centered on God and to remind us of His constant presence and provision.

To delight in the LORD, we must also be willing to seek His guidance and direction. This means being open to God's leading and being willing to follow His plans for our lives. By seeking God's guidance, we can experience the joy and peace that come from knowing that we are walking in His will. This guidance helps to keep our hearts aligned with God's will and to remind us of His constant care and provision.

Delight requires us to find joy in God's creation. It means recognizing the beauty and wonder of the world around us and finding pleasure in it. By finding joy in God's creation, we can experience a deeper and more lasting contentment. This recognition helps to keep our hearts centered on God and to remind us of His constant presence and provision.

To delight in the LORD, we must also be willing to share our joy with others. This means being open about our relationship with God and sharing the good news of His love and grace. By sharing our joy with others, we can spread God's love and encourage those around us. This sharing helps to keep our hearts aligned with God's will and to remind us of the importance of our relationship with Him.

Delight involves being grateful for the ways that God has sustained us. It means recognizing the many ways that God has provided for us and expressing our gratitude. By being grateful for God's sustenance, we can experience a deeper and more lasting joy. This gratitude helps to keep our hearts centered on God and to remind us of His constant presence and provision.

To delight in the LORD, we must also be willing to celebrate His goodness. This means taking time to praise and worship God for His love and faithfulness. By celebrating God's goodness, we can experience the joy and fulfillment that come from being in His presence. This celebration helps to keep our hearts aligned with God's will and to remind us of the importance of our relationship with Him.

Delight requires us to focus on the eternal rather than the temporary. It means finding our joy in the things that have lasting value, such as our relationship with God, our spiritual growth, and our impact on others. By focusing on the eternal, we can experience a deeper and more lasting contentment. This perspective helps to keep our hearts centered on God and to remind us of His constant presence and provision.

To delight in the LORD, we must also be willing to rest in His presence. This means taking time to be still and to experience God's peace and rest. By resting in God's presence, we can experience the joy and contentment that come from being close to Him. This rest helps to keep our hearts aligned with God's will and to remind us of His constant care and provision.

In conclusion, "Delight thyself also in the LORD" is a powerful command that emphasizes delight. Psalm 37:4 urges believers to find their greatest joy and satisfaction in God, to take pleasure in knowing Him, and to cherish His presence. Delight involves cultivating a relationship with God, trusting in His goodness, being grateful for His blessings, finding joy in His Word, serving Him and others, focusing on the eternal, surrendering our desires to Him, being patient and waiting on His timing, being open to His leading, prioritizing our relationship with Him, being joyful in His presence, seeking Him with all our hearts, finding joy in simple things, trusting Him with our future, being thankful for His presence, letting go of worries and fears, focusing on the positive aspects of our lives, serving Him with joy, being hopeful and optimistic, forgiving ourselves and others, being content with what we have, trusting Him with our desires, being joyful in His promises, seeking His guidance, finding joy in His creation, sharing our joy with others, being grateful for His sustenance, celebrating His goodness, focusing on the eternal, and resting in His presence. By embracing this command, we can experience a deep and lasting joy and fulfillment that come from knowing and loving God, and we can reflect His love and grace in our lives. In conclusion, "Delight thyself also in the LORD" is a command that calls for delight, encouraging us to find our greatest joy and satisfaction in God and to experience the fulfillment that comes from a close relationship with Him.

Chapter 7 - Departure - "Depart from evil"

Proverbs 3:7 - "Be not wise in thine own eyes: fear the LORD, and depart from evil."

This verse emphasizes departure, urging believers to turn away from wickedness and wrongdoing and to pursue a life of righteousness and reverence for God. To depart from evil means to consciously and deliberately choose to avoid sinful behaviors, thoughts, and influences, and instead to follow the path that aligns with God's will and commands. Departure in this context refers to the act of making a decisive break from sin and committing to a life that honors God. This command encourages us to recognize the dangers of evil, to seek God's wisdom and guidance, and to live in a way that reflects our respect and love for Him.

Departing from evil begins with acknowledging our own limitations and the dangers of self-reliance. The verse cautions against being "wise in thine own eyes," which means relying solely on our own understanding and judgment. This warning reminds us that our human wisdom is flawed and that we need to depend on God's guidance and wisdom to navigate life righteously. By humbling ourselves and seeking God's direction, we can avoid the pitfalls of pride and self-deception that often lead to sinful behavior.

To depart from evil, we must cultivate a healthy fear of the LORD. This fear is not about being scared of God but having a deep reverence and respect for His holiness, power, and authority. It involves recognizing that God is just and righteous and that He detests sin. By developing this reverence for God, we become more motivated to avoid evil and to live in a way that pleases Him. This fear of the LORD acts as a protective barrier, guiding us away from temptation and towards a life of integrity.

Departure from evil requires us to be vigilant and discerning. It means being aware of the influences and situations that can lead us into sin and making a conscious effort to avoid them. This vigilance involves guarding our hearts and minds, being mindful of the media we consume, the company we keep, and the environments we frequent. By being discerning, we can identify potential threats to our spiritual well-being and take proactive steps to stay clear of them.

To depart from evil, we must also be committed to personal holiness and purity. This involves striving to live according to God's standards and rejecting behaviors and attitudes that are contrary to His will. Personal holiness is about more than just outward actions; it includes the thoughts, desires, and intentions of our hearts. By seeking to purify our hearts and minds, we can align ourselves more closely with God's righteousness and depart from evil more effectively.

Departure from evil involves repentance and seeking God's forgiveness. When we recognize areas of sin in our lives, we must be willing to turn away from them and seek God's mercy. Repentance is a crucial step in departing from evil, as it involves a genuine change of heart and a commitment to living differently. By confessing our sins and seeking God's forgiveness, we can experience His grace and be empowered to live a life that honors Him.

To depart from evil, we must also embrace the transformative power of God's Word. The Bible provides us with guidance, wisdom, and instruction on how to live righteously. By studying Scripture and applying its teachings to our lives, we can gain the strength and insight needed to resist temptation and avoid sin. The Word of God acts as a lamp to our feet and a light to our path, helping us to navigate life in a way that departs from evil and honors God.

Departure from evil requires us to cultivate healthy and supportive relationships with other believers. Fellowship with other Christians provides encouragement, accountability, and support in our efforts to live righteously. By being part of a faith community, we can share our struggles, receive prayer, and find strength in the collective faith of others. This sense of community reinforces our commitment to departing from evil and helps us to stay on the path of righteousness.

To depart from evil, we must also be intentional about developing godly habits and disciplines. This includes regular prayer, Bible study, worship, and reflection. By establishing these spiritual practices as part of our daily routine, we can strengthen our relationship with God and build a solid foundation for living righteously. These habits help to keep our hearts and minds focused on God and provide the spiritual nourishment we need to resist temptation and avoid sin.

Departure from evil involves being willing to make sacrifices and to let go of things that hinder our spiritual growth. This can include ending relationships, avoiding certain activities, or giving up habits that lead us away from God. By being willing to make these sacrifices, we demonstrate our commitment to living a life that honors God. This willingness to let go of what is harmful helps to create space for God's blessings and for growth in our relationship with Him.

To depart from evil, we must also seek God's wisdom and guidance in all aspects of our lives. This means praying for discernment, seeking counsel from mature believers, and being open to the leading of the Holy Spirit. By relying on God's wisdom rather than our own understanding, we can make decisions that align with His will and avoid the pitfalls of sin. This dependence on God's guidance helps to ensure that we are walking in the path of righteousness.

Departure from evil requires us to be proactive in addressing areas of weakness and vulnerability. This involves identifying the aspects of our lives where we are most susceptible to temptation and taking steps to strengthen our defenses. This might include setting boundaries, seeking accountability, or developing new habits that support our spiritual growth. By being proactive, we can fortify our commitment to departing from evil and protect ourselves from the devil's schemes.

To depart from evil, we must also be committed to spiritual growth and development. This involves continually seeking to deepen our understanding of God's Word, to grow in our relationship with Him, and to develop our spiritual disciplines. By pursuing spiritual growth, we can strengthen our commitment to living righteously and avoid the temptations and pitfalls of sin. This continuous growth helps to keep our faith dynamic and alive and ensures that we are always moving closer to God.

Departure from evil involves being humble and recognizing our need for God's help. It means acknowledging that we cannot overcome sin on our own and that we need God's strength and guidance. By being humble, we open ourselves to God's provision and support, which empowers us to depart from evil. This humility helps us to stay reliant on God and to seek His help in times of need.

To depart from evil, we must also be vigilant in guarding our thoughts and minds. The battle against sin often begins in our minds, and by taking control of our thoughts, we can prevent sinful behaviors from taking root. This involves being mindful of what we allow into our minds, such as the media we consume and the conversations we engage in. By filling our minds with God's truth and focusing on what is pure and good, we can resist the temptations that lead to evil.

Departure from evil requires us to be patient and persistent. Overcoming sin and living righteously is a lifelong journey that requires dedication and perseverance. By being patient with ourselves and with the process, we can stay committed to our goal of departing from evil. This persistence helps us to maintain our focus on God and to continue striving for a life that honors Him.

To depart from evil, we must also be willing to forgive ourselves and others. Holding onto past mistakes and grudges can hinder our spiritual growth and keep us trapped in patterns of sin. By forgiving ourselves and others, we can release the burden of guilt and bitterness and experience the freedom that comes from God's grace. This forgiveness helps to create a clean slate, allowing us to move forward in our commitment to living righteously.

Departure from evil involves being hopeful and optimistic about our ability to change. It means believing that with God's help, we can overcome sin and live a life that honors Him. By maintaining a hopeful attitude, we can stay motivated and encouraged in our efforts to depart from evil. This hope helps to sustain us through challenges and to keep our focus on God's promises and His power to transform our lives.

To depart from evil, we must also be committed to sharing our journey with others. By being open about our struggles and victories, we can encourage and inspire those around us. Sharing our testimony of how God has helped us to depart from evil can provide hope and motivation to others who are on the same journey. This sharing helps to build a sense of community and support, reinforcing our commitment to living righteously.

Departure from evil requires us to be grateful for God's grace and forgiveness. It means recognizing that without God's mercy, we would be lost in our sin. By being thankful for God's grace, we can stay humble and reliant on Him. This gratitude helps to keep our hearts centered on God and reminds us of His constant presence and provision.

To depart from evil, we must also be willing to celebrate our progress and victories. Recognizing and celebrating the steps we have taken towards living righteously can provide motivation and encouragement. By acknowledging our growth, we can stay inspired to continue our journey of departing from evil. This celebration helps to reinforce our commitment and to keep us focused on our goal of living a life that honors God.

Departure from evil involves being accountable to others. This means seeking the support and guidance of trusted friends or mentors who can help us stay on track. By being accountable, we can receive encouragement and correction when needed, helping us to maintain our commitment to living righteously. This accountability helps to build a strong support system and reinforces our efforts to depart from evil.

To depart from evil, we must also be committed to seeking justice and righteousness in our communities. This involves standing up for what is right and working towards creating a more just and equitable world. By seeking justice, we demonstrate our commitment to living in accordance with God's will and to promoting righteousness in all areas of our lives. This commitment helps to ensure that our relationships and actions reflect our dedication to departing from evil.

Departure from evil requires us to be flexible and adaptable. It means being willing

to adjust our approaches and strategies to suit different challenges and situations. By being flexible, we can respond effectively to the devil's tactics and maintain our commitment to living righteously. This adaptability helps to ensure that we are always prepared and equipped to depart from evil.

To depart from evil, we must also be committed to living out our faith in practical ways. This involves demonstrating our commitment to God through our actions, such as showing love, kindness, and compassion to others. By living out our faith, we strengthen our commitment to departing from evil and provide a powerful witness to others. This practical expression of our faith helps to promote God's kingdom and to protect us from the devil's schemes.

Departure from evil involves being mindful of our physical and emotional well-being. Taking care of our bodies and minds by getting enough rest, eating well, and seeking support when needed helps us to better manage our stress and responsibilities. By prioritizing our health, we can stay balanced and resilient in our efforts to depart from evil. This mindfulness helps to ensure that we are in a strong position to resist temptation and to live a life that honors God.

To depart from evil, we must also be committed to seeking God's wisdom and guidance in all aspects of our lives. This means praying for discernment, seeking counsel from mature believers, and being open to the leading of the Holy Spirit. By relying on God's wisdom rather than our own understanding, we can make decisions that align with His will and avoid the pitfalls of sin. This dependence on God's guidance helps to ensure that we are walking in the path of righteousness.

Departure from evil requires us to be proactive in addressing areas of weakness and vulnerability. This involves identifying the aspects of our lives where we are most susceptible to temptation and taking steps to strengthen our defenses. This might include setting boundaries, seeking accountability, or developing new habits that support our spiritual growth. By being proactive, we can fortify our commitment to departing from evil and protect ourselves from the devil's schemes.

To depart from evil, we must also be committed to spiritual growth and development. This involves continually seeking to deepen our understanding of God's Word, to grow in our relationship with Him, and to develop our spiritual disciplines. By pursuing spiritual growth, we can strengthen our commitment to living righteously and avoid the temptations and pitfalls of sin. This continuous growth helps to keep our faith dynamic and alive and ensures that we are always moving closer to God.

In conclusion, "Depart from evil" is a powerful command that emphasizes departure. Proverbs 3:7 urges believers to turn away from wickedness and wrongdoing and to pursue a life of righteousness and reverence for God. Departure involves recognizing our limitations, cultivating a fear of the LORD, being vigilant and discerning, striving for personal holiness, repenting and seeking God's forgiveness, embracing God's Word, cultivating supportive relationships, developing godly habits, making sacrifices, seeking God's wisdom, addressing weaknesses, pursuing spiritual growth, being humble, guarding our thoughts, being patient and persistent, forgiving ourselves and others, being hopeful, sharing our journey, being grateful for God's grace, celebrating progress, being accountable, seeking justice, being flexible, living out our faith practically, being mindful of our well-being, and being proactive. By embracing this command, we can ensure that our lives reflect our commitment to departing from evil and living a life that honors God. In conclusion, "Depart from evil" is a command that calls for departure, encouraging us to turn away from sin and to pursue a life of righteousness and reverence for God.

Chapter 8 - Draw - "Draw nigh to God"

James 4:8 - "Draw nigh to God, and he will draw nigh to you. Cleanse your hands, ye sinners; and purify your hearts, ye double minded."
This verse emphasizes the action of drawing near to God, urging believers to seek a close and intimate relationship with Him. To draw nigh to God means to actively move towards Him, to seek His presence, and to foster a deeper connection with Him through our thoughts, actions, and hearts. Drawing near in this context refers to the intentional and persistent effort to build and maintain a relationship with God, marked by purity, sincerity, and devotion. This command encourages us to cleanse ourselves from sin, to focus our hearts and minds on God, and to trust that as we move closer to Him, He will respond by drawing closer to us, strengthening our bond with Him.

Drawing near to God begins with a sincere desire to know Him and to be in His presence. This involves setting aside time each day to pray, read the Bible, and meditate on His Word. By making these practices a regular part of our routine, we can cultivate a habit of seeking God and growing closer to Him. This daily commitment helps to center our lives around God and to prioritize our relationship with Him above all else.

To draw nigh to God, we must also be willing to repent of our sins and seek His forgiveness. The verse calls us to "cleanse your hands, ye sinners; and purify your hearts, ye double minded." This cleansing and purification involve acknowledging our wrongdoings, feeling genuine remorse, and turning away from sinful behaviors. By confessing our sins and asking for God's forgiveness, we can remove the barriers that separate us from Him and experience the cleansing power of His grace. This repentance is a crucial step in drawing near to God, as it demonstrates our desire to live a life that honors Him.

Drawing near to God requires us to cultivate a pure heart and a sincere faith. It means being honest and transparent in our relationship with God, bringing our true selves before Him without pretense or hypocrisy. By seeking to purify our hearts and align our thoughts and desires with God's will, we can build a deeper and more authentic connection with Him. This sincerity helps to foster a relationship based on trust and mutual love, allowing us to experience God's presence more fully.

To draw nigh to God, we must also be diligent in our pursuit of holiness. This involves striving to live according to God's standards and seeking to reflect His character in our actions and attitudes. By living a life of integrity, kindness, and compassion, we can draw closer to God and become more like Him. This pursuit of holiness is a lifelong journey that requires dedication and perseverance, but it is essential for deepening our relationship with God.

Drawing near to God involves seeking His guidance and direction in all aspects of our lives. It means bringing our decisions, plans, and concerns to Him in prayer and being open to His leading. By relying on God's wisdom rather than our own understanding, we can make choices that align with His will and draw us closer to Him. This dependence on God helps to strengthen our faith and to cultivate a deeper sense of trust and reliance on Him.

To draw nigh to God, we must also immerse ourselves in His Word. The Bible is a rich source of knowledge, encouragement, and instruction, and by studying it, we can gain a deeper understanding of God's character and His will for our lives. By meditating on Scripture and applying its teachings to our daily lives, we can draw closer to God and experience His presence in new and profound ways. This engagement with God's Word helps to nourish our souls and to keep our hearts aligned with His purposes.

Drawing near to God requires us to worship Him with a genuine and thankful heart. Worship is an expression of our love and adoration for God, and it helps to draw us into His presence. By praising God for His goodness, faithfulness, and grace, we can experience a deeper sense of connection with Him. This worship can take many forms, including singing, praying, and reflecting on God's attributes. By making worship a regular part of our lives, we can cultivate a heart of gratitude and devotion that draws us closer to God.

To draw nigh to God, we must also cultivate a spirit of humility and dependence. It means recognizing our need for God's grace and acknowledging that we cannot navigate life on our own. By humbling ourselves before God and seeking His help, we open ourselves to His guidance and support. This humility allows us to experience the fullness of God's love and to draw closer to Him in our daily walk.

Drawing near to God involves seeking fellowship with other believers. Being part of a faith community provides encouragement, accountability, and support in our spiritual journey. By sharing our experiences, challenges, and victories with others, we can grow together in our relationship with God. This sense of community helps to strengthen our faith and to draw us closer to God as we support and uplift one another.

To draw nigh to God, we must also be intentional about serving others. Jesus taught that serving others is a way to demonstrate our love for God and to reflect His character. By using our gifts and talents to bless those around us, we can draw closer to God and experience His presence in our acts of service. This service helps to align our hearts with God's purposes and to cultivate a spirit of generosity and compassion.

Drawing near to God requires us to be patient and persistent in our pursuit of Him. Building a deep and meaningful relationship with God takes time and effort, and it requires us to remain steadfast in our commitment. By being patient and persistent, we can overcome the obstacles and distractions that seek to pull us away from God. This perseverance helps to strengthen our faith and to deepen our relationship with Him.

To draw nigh to God, we must also be open to the work of the Holy Spirit in our lives. The Holy Spirit is our guide, comforter, and teacher, and by being sensitive to His leading, we can draw closer to God. This openness involves being willing to listen to the Spirit's promptings and to follow His direction. By allowing the Holy Spirit to work in us and through us, we can experience a deeper and more intimate relationship with God. Drawing near to God involves being grateful for His presence and blessings in our lives. It means recognizing the many ways that God is at work in us and around us and expressing our gratitude for His goodness. By cultivating a heart of thankfulness, we can draw closer to God and experience His joy and peace. This gratitude helps to keep our hearts centered on God and to remind us of His constant care and provision.

To draw nigh to God, we must also be willing to let go of the things that hinder our relationship with Him. This includes letting go of sinful behaviors, unhealthy relationships, and distractions that pull us away from God. By surrendering these things to God, we can create space in our lives for His presence and work. This surrender helps to purify our hearts and to draw us closer to God in our daily walk.

Drawing near to God requires us to focus on the eternal rather than the temporary. It means setting our hearts and minds on the things of God and seeking to live in light of eternity. By focusing on the eternal, we can draw closer to God and experience the peace and fulfillment that come from living for His kingdom. This eternal perspective helps to keep our hearts aligned with God's purposes and to draw us closer to Him.

To draw nigh to God, we must also be willing to trust Him with our future. It means believing that God has good plans for our lives and being willing to follow His leading. By trusting God with our future, we can draw closer to Him and experience the joy and peace that come from knowing that He is in control. This trust helps to strengthen our relationship with God and to deepen our faith.

Drawing near to God involves being joyful in His presence. It means finding pleasure in spending time with God, worshiping Him, and experiencing His love. By being joyful in God's presence, we can draw closer to Him and experience a deeper and more fulfilling relationship. This joy helps to strengthen our faith and to keep our hearts centered on God. To draw nigh to God, we must also seek to live in obedience to His commands. Obedience is a way to demonstrate our love for God and to align our lives with His will. By living in obedience, we can draw closer to God and experience the blessings that come from following His ways. This obedience helps to strengthen our relationship with God and to deepen our connection with Him.

Drawing near to God requires us to be intentional about seeking His presence in all aspects of our lives. This means inviting God into our daily routines, decisions, and activities. By seeking God's presence in everything we do, we can draw closer to Him and experience His guidance and support. This intentionality helps to strengthen our relationship with God and to keep our hearts aligned with His will.

To draw nigh to God, we must also be committed to personal growth and spiritual development. This involves continually seeking to deepen our understanding of God's Word, to grow in our relationship with Him, and to develop our spiritual disciplines. By pursuing spiritual growth, we can draw closer to God and experience the fullness of His presence in our lives. This commitment to growth helps to strengthen our faith and to deepen our connection with God.

Drawing near to God involves being flexible and adaptable in our relationship with Him. It means being willing to adjust our approaches and strategies to suit different challenges and situations. By being flexible, we can respond effectively to the changes and challenges we face and maintain our connection with God. This adaptability helps to ensure that we are always moving closer to God, regardless of our circumstances.

To draw nigh to God, we must also be committed to living out our faith in practical ways. This involves demonstrating our commitment to God through our actions, such as showing love, kindness, and compassion to others. By living out our faith, we can draw closer to God and experience His presence in our daily lives. This practical expression of our faith helps to promote God's kingdom and to strengthen our relationship with Him.

Drawing near to God requires us to be mindful of our physical and emotional well-being. Taking care of our bodies and minds by getting enough rest, eating well, and seeking support when needed helps us to better manage our stress and responsibilities. By prioritizing our health, we can stay balanced and resilient in our efforts to draw closer to God. This mindfulness helps to ensure that we are in a strong position to maintain our connection with Him.

To draw nigh to God, we must also be committed to seeking His wisdom and guidance in all aspects of our lives. This means praying for discernment, seeking counsel from mature believers, and being open to the leading of the Holy Spirit. By relying on God's wisdom rather than our own understanding, we can make decisions that align with His will and draw us closer to Him. This dependence on God's guidance helps to ensure that we are walking in the path of righteousness.

Drawing near to God requires us to be proactive in addressing areas of weakness and vulnerability. This involves identifying the aspects of our lives where we are most susceptible to temptation and taking steps to strengthen our defenses. This might include setting boundaries, seeking accountability, or developing new habits that support our spiritual growth. By being proactive, we can fortify our commitment to drawing near to God and protect ourselves from the devil's schemes.

In conclusion, "Draw nigh to God" is a powerful command that emphasizes drawing near. James 4:8 urges believers to seek a close and intimate relationship with God, to cleanse themselves from sin, and to purify their hearts. Drawing near involves a sincere desire to know

God, repentance, cultivating a pure heart, pursuing holiness, seeking God's guidance, immersing ourselves in His Word, worshiping Him, cultivating humility, seeking fellowship, serving others, being patient and persistent, being open to the Holy Spirit, being grateful, letting go of hindrances, focusing on the eternal, trusting God with our future, being joyful in His presence, living in obedience, seeking His presence, pursuing personal growth, being flexible, living out our faith practically, being mindful of our well-being, seeking His wisdom, and addressing weaknesses. By embracing this command, we can ensure that our lives reflect our commitment to drawing near to God and experiencing the fullness of His presence. In conclusion, "Draw nigh to God" is a command that calls for drawing near, encouraging us to seek a close and intimate relationship with God and to experience the joy and fulfillment that come from knowing and loving Him.

Chapter 9 - Doing "Do good"

Psalm 34:14 - "Depart from evil, and do good; seek peace, and pursue it."

This verse emphasizes doing, urging believers to actively engage in positive and righteous actions. To do good means to live a life characterized by kindness, generosity, and integrity, making choices that reflect the values and teachings of God. Doing good involves intentionally seeking out opportunities to help others, to promote peace, and to contribute positively to the world around us. This command encourages us to move beyond merely avoiding evil and to proactively pursue actions that demonstrate our faith and commitment to God's principles.

Doing good begins with a conscious decision to depart from evil. This means recognizing and rejecting behaviors, thoughts, and influences that lead us away from God. By turning away from sin, we create space in our lives for positive and righteous actions. Departing from evil is not just about avoiding wrongdoing; it also involves a commitment to living in a way that honors God and reflects His character. This decision to depart from evil sets the foundation for a life of doing good.

To do good, we must cultivate a heart of compassion and empathy. This involves being sensitive to the needs and struggles of others and being willing to take action to help them. Compassion drives us to reach out to those who are hurting, to offer support, and to make a positive difference in their lives. By developing a compassionate heart, we can be more effective in our efforts to do good and to reflect God's love in our actions.

Doing good requires us to be generous with our time, resources, and talents. It means being willing to share what we have with others and to use our abilities to benefit those around us. Generosity is a key aspect of doing good, as it demonstrates our willingness to put the needs of others before our own and to contribute to the well-being of our community. By practicing generosity, we can create a ripple effect of kindness and positive change.

To do good, we must also seek peace and pursue it. This involves actively working to resolve conflicts, to promote understanding, and to foster harmony in our relationships. Seeking peace means being a peacemaker, someone who strives to bring people together and to build bridges of reconciliation. By pursuing peace, we can create an environment where goodness can flourish and where people can experience the love and grace of God.

Doing good involves being honest and trustworthy. It means living with integrity, being truthful in our words and actions, and being reliable in our commitments. Honesty builds trust and credibility, which are essential for creating positive and healthy relationships. By being honest and trustworthy, we can set a positive example for others and contribute to a culture of integrity and respect.

To do good, we must also be kind and considerate in our interactions with others. This means treating people with respect, being polite, and showing kindness in our words and actions. Kindness can have a powerful impact on those around us, creating a positive and supportive atmosphere. By being kind and considerate, we can demonstrate the love of God and make a meaningful difference in the lives of others.

Doing good requires us to be proactive in seeking out opportunities to help others. This means looking for ways to serve, to volunteer, and to make a positive impact in our community. By being proactive, we can identify needs and take action to address them, rather than waiting for opportunities to come to us. This proactive approach helps to ensure that we are actively engaged in doing good and making a difference.

To do good, we must also be patient and persistent. Doing good often involves facing challenges and obstacles, and it requires us to be steadfast in our commitment. Patience allows us to persevere in our efforts, even when progress is slow or difficult. By being patient and persistent, we can continue to make a positive impact and to uphold our commitment to doing good.

Doing good involves being humble and willing to put others before ourselves. It means recognizing that we are not the center of the universe and that our actions should be focused on serving and benefiting others. Humility allows us to see the value and worth of those around us and to act in ways that uplift and support them. By being humble, we can create a culture of selflessness and generosity.

To do good, we must also be courageous and willing to stand up for what is right. This means speaking out against injustice, defending the vulnerable, and taking action to promote fairness and equality. Courage is essential for doing good, as it allows us to take bold and necessary steps to create positive change. By being courageous, we can make a meaningful impact and contribute to a more just and compassionate world.

Doing good requires us to be thoughtful and intentional in our actions. It means considering the potential impact of our choices and striving to make decisions that benefit others and reflect God's values. Thoughtfulness helps us to act with wisdom and discernment, ensuring that our efforts to do good are effective and meaningful. By being intentional, we can maximize the positive impact of our actions.

To do good, we must also be forgiving and willing to extend grace to others. This involves letting go of grudges, offering forgiveness, and seeking reconciliation in our relationships. Forgiveness is a powerful act of goodness, as it promotes healing and restores broken relationships. By being forgiving, we can create an environment where love and grace can thrive.

Doing good involves being grateful for the blessings and opportunities we have. Gratitude helps us to appreciate what we have and to be generous in sharing it with others. By cultivating a thankful heart, we can approach our efforts to do good with a positive and joyful attitude. Gratitude also helps us to recognize the goodness in our lives and to be motivated to spread that goodness to others.

To do good, we must also be open to learning and growing. This means being willing to seek out new knowledge, to listen to others, and to adapt our actions based on what we learn. Continuous learning helps us to improve our ability to do good and to make a positive impact. By being open to growth, we can become more effective and compassionate in our efforts.

Doing good requires us to be flexible and adaptable. It means being willing to adjust our plans and approaches to meet the needs of different situations and people. Flexibility allows us to respond effectively to changing circumstances and to find the best ways to serve and help others. By being adaptable, we can ensure that our efforts to do good are relevant and impactful.

To do good, we must also be mindful of our well-being. Taking care of our physical, emotional, and spiritual health allows us to be more effective in our efforts to help others. By prioritizing self-care, we can ensure that we have the energy and resilience needed to continue doing good. This mindfulness helps us to sustain our commitment to positive action.

Doing good involves being positive and hopeful. It means maintaining a positive outlook and believing in the potential for good in the world. Hopefulness helps us to stay motivated and to inspire others to join us in our efforts. By being positive and hopeful, we can create a culture of optimism and possibility.

To do good, we must also be responsible and accountable. This means taking ownership of our actions and being willing to accept the consequences of our choices. Responsibility helps us to act with integrity and to be reliable in our commitments. By being accountable, we can build trust and credibility in our efforts to do good.

Doing good requires us to be respectful and considerate of others' perspectives and experiences. It means listening to and valuing the voices of those around us. Respect helps to create an inclusive and supportive environment where everyone feels valued and heard. By being respectful, we can foster a culture of kindness and mutual support.

To do good, we must also be creative and innovative. This involves finding new and effective ways to address challenges and to make a positive impact. Creativity allows us to think outside the box and to develop unique solutions to problems. By being innovative, we can enhance our ability to do good and to create lasting change.

Doing good involves being committed to long-term impact. It means thinking beyond immediate actions and considering the lasting effects of our efforts. Long-term commitment helps us to create sustainable change and to make a meaningful difference in the lives of others. By being dedicated to lasting impact, we can ensure that our efforts to do good are truly transformative.

To do good, we must also be inspired by the example of Jesus. Jesus' life and teachings provide a perfect model of goodness, kindness, and compassion. By following His example, we can be motivated and guided in our efforts to do good. This inspiration helps us to stay focused on our goal of living a life that honors God and benefits others.

Doing good requires us to be driven by love. Love is the foundation of all good actions, motivating us to care for others and to seek their well-being. By letting love guide our actions, we can ensure that our efforts to do good are genuine and heartfelt. This love helps to create a powerful and lasting impact.

In conclusion, "Do good" is a powerful command that emphasizes doing. Psalm 34:14 urges believers to actively engage in positive and righteous actions, to depart from evil, and to seek peace. Doing good involves making a conscious decision to reject sin, cultivating a heart of compassion, being generous, seeking peace, being honest and trustworthy, being kind and considerate, being proactive, being patient and persistent, being humble, being courageous, being thoughtful and intentional, being forgiving, being grateful, being open to learning, being flexible, being mindful of our well-being, being positive and hopeful, being responsible and accountable, being respectful, being creative and innovative, being committed to long-term impact, being inspired by Jesus' example, and being driven by love. By embracing this command, we can ensure that our lives reflect our commitment to doing good and making a positive impact on the world around us. In conclusion, "Do good" is a command that calls for active engagement in positive and righteous actions, encouraging us to live a life that honors God and benefits others.

Chapter 10 - Denial - "Deny yourself"

Luke 9:23 - "And he said to them all, If any man will come after me, let him deny himself, and take up his cross daily, and follow me."

This verse emphasizes denial, urging believers to reject selfish desires and to commit to a life of selflessness and sacrifice in following Jesus. To deny oneself means to put aside personal ambitions, comforts, and desires in order to prioritize the will of God and the teachings of Jesus. Denial in this context refers to the deliberate and intentional decision to live in a way that reflects Jesus' example of humility, sacrifice, and service. This command encourages us to embrace a lifestyle of self-denial, taking up our cross daily, and dedicating ourselves to the path that Jesus has set before us.

Denying yourself begins with the recognition that following Jesus requires a complete transformation of priorities. It involves a fundamental shift from living for oneself to living for God. This means making decisions that reflect God's values rather than our own desires. By choosing to deny ourselves, we acknowledge that our lives are not our own, but belong to God. This mindset helps us to align our actions and attitudes with the teachings of Jesus and to live in a way that honors Him.

To deny yourself, you must be willing to let go of personal ambitions and desires that conflict with God's will. This means being open to surrendering your plans and goals to God and trusting that His plans are better than your own. By letting go of self-centered ambitions, you make room for God's purposes to unfold in your life. This surrender is a key aspect of self-denial, as it demonstrates a willingness to prioritize God's will above all else.

Denying yourself requires a daily commitment to take up your cross. This means being prepared to face challenges, hardships, and sacrifices for the sake of following Jesus. Taking up your cross daily involves a readiness to endure difficulties and to remain steadfast in your faith, even when it is costly or uncomfortable. By embracing this daily commitment, you demonstrate your dedication to following Jesus and your willingness to share in His sufferings.

To deny yourself, you must also cultivate a heart of humility. Humility involves recognizing your own limitations and weaknesses and being willing to put the needs of others before your own. By developing a humble heart, you can more effectively serve others and reflect the character of Jesus in your actions. This humility helps to break down the barriers of pride and self-centeredness that can hinder your relationship with God and others.

Denying yourself involves being willing to serve others selflessly. This means looking for opportunities to help and support those around you, even when it requires personal sacrifice. By serving others, you demonstrate the love of Jesus and fulfill His command to love your neighbor as yourself. This selfless service helps to cultivate a spirit of generosity and compassion, which are essential aspects of self-denial.

To deny yourself, you must also be willing to practice self-discipline. This involves controlling your desires and impulses and making choices that reflect your commitment to following Jesus. Self-discipline helps you to resist temptations and to stay focused on the path that God has set before you. By practicing self-discipline, you can develop the strength and resilience needed to live a life of self-denial.

Denying yourself requires a deep and abiding trust in God. It means believing that God is faithful and that He will provide for your needs as you seek to follow Him. This trust allows you to let go of the need to control your own life and to rely on God's guidance and provision. By trusting in God, you can experience the peace and security that come from knowing that He is in control.

To deny yourself, you must also be committed to living a life of integrity and righteousness. This means making choices that reflect God's standards and striving to live in a way that is pleasing to Him.

By prioritizing righteousness, you demonstrate your commitment to following Jesus and your desire to live according to His teachings. This commitment to integrity helps to strengthen your relationship with God and to build a strong foundation for your faith.

Denying yourself involves being willing to endure suffering and hardship for the sake of following Jesus. This means accepting that the path of discipleship may involve trials and challenges, but remaining steadfast in your faith regardless. By embracing suffering as a part of your journey, you can develop a deeper understanding of Jesus' sacrifice and grow closer to Him. This willingness to endure hardship is a crucial aspect of self-denial, as it demonstrates your commitment to following Jesus no matter the cost.

To deny yourself, you must also be open to the work of the Holy Spirit in your life. The Holy Spirit provides guidance, comfort, and strength as you seek to follow Jesus and live a life of self-denial. By being sensitive to the Spirit's leading, you can receive the support and encouragement needed to stay on the path of discipleship. This openness to the Holy Spirit helps to ensure that you are living in accordance with God's will.

Denying yourself requires a commitment to personal growth and spiritual development. This involves continually seeking to deepen your understanding of God's Word, to grow in your relationship with Him, and to develop your spiritual disciplines. By pursuing spiritual growth, you can strengthen your commitment to self-denial and enhance your ability to follow Jesus faithfully. This dedication to growth helps to ensure that your faith remains dynamic and alive.

To deny yourself, you must also be willing to let go of material possessions and comforts that can distract you from following Jesus. This means being willing to live simply and to prioritize spiritual riches over material wealth. By letting go of the pursuit of material gain, you can focus more fully on your relationship with God and your commitment to following Him. This simplicity helps to cultivate a spirit of contentment and gratitude, which are essential for a life of self-denial.

Denying yourself involves being willing to forgive others and to seek reconciliation in your relationships. Forgiveness is a powerful act of self-denial, as it requires letting go of grudges and choosing to extend grace and mercy. By practicing forgiveness, you can experience the healing and freedom that come from releasing bitterness and resentment. This commitment to reconciliation helps to build strong and healthy relationships, reflecting the love of Jesus.

To deny yourself, you must also be committed to sharing the gospel and making disciples. This means being willing to speak about your faith and to invest in the spiritual growth of others. By prioritizing evangelism and discipleship, you demonstrate your commitment to following Jesus' command to make disciples of all nations. This dedication to sharing the gospel helps to ensure that your life is focused on advancing God's kingdom.

Denying yourself requires a willingness to embrace change and to be adaptable in your walk with God. This means being open to new opportunities and experiences that God may bring into your life. By being flexible and willing to step out of your comfort zone, you can grow in your faith and discover new ways to serve and follow Jesus. This adaptability helps to ensure that your journey of self-denial remains dynamic and responsive to God's leading.

To deny yourself, you must also be committed to prayer and seeking God's guidance in all aspects of your life. Prayer is a vital aspect of self-denial, as it connects you to God's presence and provides the strength and wisdom needed to follow Him. By making prayer a regular part of your routine, you can deepen your relationship with God and receive the support needed to live a life of self-denial.

Denying yourself involves being grateful for the blessings and opportunities that God has given you. Gratitude helps to cultivate a positive and joyful attitude, even in the midst of challenges and sacrifices. By focusing on the goodness of God and expressing thankfulness, you can stay motivated and encouraged in your journey of self-denial. This gratitude helps to ensure that your heart remains centered on God and His provision.

To deny yourself, you must also be willing to invest in the well-being of others. This means using your time, resources, and talents to serve and support those around you. By prioritizing the needs of others, you demonstrate the love of Jesus and fulfill His command to love your neighbor as yourself. This commitment to serving others helps to cultivate a spirit of generosity and compassion, which are essential aspects of self-denial.

Denying yourself requires a commitment to honesty and transparency in your relationships. This means being truthful in your words and actions and being willing to admit your mistakes and seek forgiveness. By practicing honesty, you build trust and credibility in your relationships, reflecting the integrity of Jesus. This commitment to truth helps to ensure that your interactions with others are genuine and authentic.

To deny yourself, you must also be willing to seek justice and to stand up for what is right. This means being willing to speak out against injustice and to take action to promote fairness and equality. By prioritizing justice, you demonstrate your commitment to living according to God's values and to making a positive impact in the world. This dedication to justice helps to ensure that your life reflects the principles of God's kingdom.

Denying yourself involves being mindful of your physical and emotional well-being. Taking care of your body and mind by getting enough rest, eating well, and seeking support when needed helps you to better manage the demands of following Jesus. By prioritizing self-care, you can ensure that you have the energy and resilience needed to continue your journey of self-denial. This mindfulness helps to sustain your commitment to following Jesus.

To deny yourself, you must also be willing to seek wisdom and guidance from others. This means being open to learning from the experiences and insights of mature believers. By seeking counsel and mentorship, you can gain valuable support and encouragement in your journey of self-denial. This openness to guidance helps to ensure that you are growing and maturing in your faith.

Denying yourself requires a commitment to living out your faith in practical ways. This involves demonstrating your commitment to God through your actions, such as showing love, kindness, and compassion to others. By living out your faith, you can make a positive impact and provide a powerful witness to those

around you. This practical expression of your faith helps to ensure that your life reflects the principles of self-denial.

To deny yourself, you must also be willing to embrace simplicity and contentment. This means finding joy and satisfaction in the simple things and being content with what you have. By focusing on the blessings and opportunities that God has given you, you can cultivate a spirit of gratitude and contentment. This simplicity helps to ensure that your heart remains centered on God and His provision.

Denying yourself involves being committed to seeking peace in your relationships. This means actively working to resolve conflicts and to promote understanding and reconciliation. By prioritizing peace, you demonstrate the love of Jesus and fulfill His command to be peacemakers. This commitment to peace helps to build strong and healthy relationships and to create a supportive and loving community.

To deny yourself, you must also be willing to trust God with your future. This means believing that God has good plans for your life and being willing to follow His leading. By trusting God with your future, you can experience the peace and security that come from knowing that He is in control. This trust helps to strengthen your relationship with God and to deepen your faith.

Denying yourself requires a willingness to let go of the past and to focus on the future. This means releasing any regrets, mistakes, or hurts and embracing the new opportunities that God has for you. By letting go of the past, you can move forward with a sense of hope and anticipation for what God has in store. This focus on the future helps to sustain your commitment to self-denial.

In conclusion, "Deny yourself" is a powerful command that emphasizes denial. Luke 9:23 urges believers to reject selfish desires, to take up their cross daily, and to follow Jesus. Denial involves a fundamental shift from living for oneself to living for God, letting go of personal ambitions, practicing humility, serving others, practicing self-discipline, trusting in God's provision, living with integrity, enduring hardship, being open to the Holy Spirit, pursuing spiritual growth, letting go of materialism, practicing forgiveness, sharing the gospel, being adaptable, committing to prayer, expressing gratitude, investing in others, practicing honesty, seeking justice, prioritizing self-care, seeking wisdom, living out faith practically, embracing simplicity, seeking peace, trusting God with the future, and letting go of the past. By embracing this command, we can ensure that our lives reflect our commitment to self-denial and to following Jesus. In conclusion, "Deny yourself" is a command that calls for denial, encouraging us to live a life of selflessness, sacrifice, and dedication to the teachings of Jesus.

Chapter 11 – Distinction - "Do not be conformed to this world"

Romans 12:2 - "And be not conformed to this world: but be ye transformed by the renewing of your mind, that ye may prove what is that good, and acceptable, and perfect, will of God."

This verse emphasizes distinction, urging believers to resist the pressures and influences of the world and instead to seek transformation through the renewal of their minds. To not be conformed to this world means to avoid adopting the values, behaviors, and attitudes that are prevalent in society but contrary to God's will. Distinction in this context refers to the deliberate choice to live differently from the world, to stand out as followers of Christ, and to reflect God's character in all aspects of life. This command encourages us to pursue spiritual growth, to cultivate a godly mindset, and to live in a way that honors God and demonstrates His good and perfect will. Not conforming to this world begins with understanding the difference between the world's values and God's values. The world often promotes selfishness, materialism, and moral relativism, while God calls us to selflessness, contentment, and absolute truth. By recognizing these differences, we can be more discerning about the influences we allow into our lives. This discernment helps us to make choices that align with God's will and to avoid being swayed by worldly pressures.

To not be conformed to this world, we must cultivate a renewed mind. This involves filling our minds with God's Word, seeking His wisdom, and allowing the Holy Spirit to transform our thinking. By regularly reading and studying the Bible, we can gain a deeper understanding of God's character and His will for our lives. This engagement with Scripture helps to reshape our thoughts and attitudes, making them more aligned with God's truth. The renewal of our minds is a continuous process that requires dedication and intentionality, but it is essential for living a life that is distinct from the world.

Resisting conformity to the world requires us to develop strong convictions based on biblical principles. This means having a clear understanding of what we believe and why we believe it. By grounding ourselves in the truth of God's Word, we can stand firm in our faith and resist the pressure to conform to societal norms that contradict our beliefs. Strong convictions provide a solid foundation for our actions and decisions, helping us to live with integrity and purpose.

To not be conformed to this world, we must also be vigilant about the influences we allow into our lives. This includes being mindful of the media we consume, the relationships we cultivate, and the environments we frequent. By carefully selecting what we watch, read, and listen to, we can protect our minds from negative influences and fill them with positive, godly content. Surrounding ourselves with like-minded believers who encourage and support our faith can also help us to stay strong and resist worldly pressures.

Living a life of distinction involves actively pursuing spiritual growth and maturity. This means seeking to deepen our relationship with God through prayer, worship, and fellowship with other believers. By prioritizing our spiritual development, we can become more attuned to God's voice and more responsive to His leading. Spiritual growth helps us to become more like Christ, reflecting His love, grace, and truth in our daily lives. This transformation not only sets us apart from the world but also serves as a powerful witness to others.

To not be conformed to this world, we must also be willing to take a stand for our faith. This means being bold and courageous in living out our beliefs, even when it is unpopular or difficult. Standing up for what is right requires strength and conviction, but it is essential for maintaining our distinctiveness as followers of Christ. By being vocal about our faith and living according to our principles, we can inspire others and bring glory to God. Living a life of distinction involves making choices that honor God in all areas of our lives. This includes our relationships, work, finances, and leisure activities. By seeking to glorify God in everything we do, we demonstrate our commitment to living according to His will. This holistic approach to faith ensures that our distinctiveness is evident in every aspect of our lives, not just in our words but also in our actions.

To not be conformed to this world, we must also cultivate a heart of humility and dependence on God. This means recognizing our own limitations and relying on God's strength and wisdom. Humility allows us to submit to God's authority and to seek His guidance in all things. By acknowledging our need for God, we can avoid the pride and self-reliance that often lead to conformity with the world. Dependence on God helps us to stay focused on His will and to live a life that is pleasing to Him. Resisting conformity to the world requires us to be intentional about our spiritual disciplines. This includes regular prayer, Bible study, worship, and reflection. By making these practices a priority, we can strengthen our relationship with God and stay grounded in His truth. Spiritual disciplines help us to remain focused on our faith and to cultivate a mindset that is distinct from the world. They provide the spiritual nourishment we need to resist worldly pressures and to live a life that honors God.

To not be conformed to this world, we must also be committed to serving others. Jesus taught that the greatest commandment is to love God and to love our neighbors as ourselves. By serving others with humility and compassion, we reflect God's love and demonstrate our distinctiveness as His followers. Service to others helps to break down the barriers of selfishness and materialism that characterize the world, allowing us to live out our faith in practical and meaningful ways.

Living a life of distinction involves being grateful for the blessings and opportunities that God has given us. Gratitude helps us to maintain a positive and joyful attitude, even in the face of challenges and difficulties. By focusing on the goodness of God and expressing thankfulness, we can stay motivated and encouraged in our journey of faith. Gratitude also helps us to recognize the many ways that God is at work in our lives, reminding us of His constant presence and provision.

To not be conformed to this world, we must also be willing to make sacrifices for the sake of our faith. This means being prepared to give up certain comforts, conveniences, or opportunities that conflict with our commitment to God. Sacrifice is a key aspect of living a life of distinction, as it demonstrates our willingness to prioritize God's will above our own desires. By making sacrifices, we show that our faith is more important than worldly gain, and we strengthen our resolve to live according to God's principles. Resisting conformity to the world requires us to be patient and persistent in our pursuit of God's will. Transformation and spiritual growth take time, and it is important to remain steadfast in our commitment to following Jesus. Patience allows us to trust in God's timing and to persevere through challenges, knowing that He is at work in our lives. Persistence helps us to stay focused on our goal of living a life that is distinct from the world, even when it is difficult or discouraging.

To not be conformed to this world, we must also seek to be peacemakers. Jesus called us to be agents of peace and reconciliation in a world that is often marked by conflict and division. By promoting peace and seeking to resolve conflicts, we demonstrate our commitment to living according to God's will. Peacemaking requires us to be compassionate, understanding, and willing to forgive. It helps to create an environment where God's love and truth can flourish, setting us apart as His followers. Living a life of distinction involves being honest and trustworthy in all our dealings. Integrity is a key characteristic of a godly life, and it helps to build trust and credibility with others. By being truthful and reliable, we reflect God's character and set a positive example for those around us. Honesty helps to distinguish us from the world, where deceit and dishonesty are often prevalent.

To not be conformed to this world, we must also be committed to continuous learning and growth. This means seeking to deepen our understanding of God's Word, to grow in our relationship with Him, and to develop our spiritual disciplines. By pursuing ongoing spiritual education, we can stay grounded in God's truth and remain resilient against worldly influences. Continuous learning helps us to stay sharp and prepared for the challenges we face in living a life that is distinct from the world.

Resisting conformity to the world requires us to be creative and innovative in finding ways to live out our faith. This means thinking outside the box and finding unique solutions to the challenges we face. Creativity allows us to adapt to changing circumstances and to find new ways to demonstrate our distinctiveness as followers of Christ. By being innovative, we can enhance our ability to live according to God's principles and to make a positive impact in the world.

To not be conformed to this world, we must also be committed to building strong and supportive relationships with other believers. Fellowship with other Christians provides encouragement, accountability, and support in our journey of faith. By sharing our experiences and challenges with others, we can grow together and strengthen our resolve to live a life that honors God. Strong relationships help to create a sense of community and belonging, which are essential for resisting worldly pressures.

Living a life of distinction involves being generous with our time, resources, and talents. Generosity reflects God's character and demonstrates our commitment to living according to His principles. By being willing to share what we have with others, we can make a positive impact and show the love of Christ in practical ways. Generosity helps to counteract the materialism and selfishness that characterize the world, setting us apart as followers of Jesus.

To not be conformed to this world, we must also be committed to practicing forgiveness and reconciliation. This means being willing to let go of grudges and to seek healing in our relationships. Forgiveness is a powerful act of distinction, as it reflects God's grace and mercy. By practicing forgiveness, we can create an environment of love and compassion, which helps to distinguish us from the world.

Resisting conformity to the world requires us to be flexible and adaptable in our faith journey. This means being open to new experiences and willing to adjust our approaches as needed. Flexibility allows us to respond effectively to the challenges we face and to remain resilient in our commitment to living a life that honors God. By being adaptable, we can stay focused on our goal of distinction, even in the face of changing circumstances.

Living a life of distinction involves being committed to prayer and seeking God's guidance in all aspects of our lives. Prayer is a vital aspect of resisting conformity to the world, as it connects us to God's presence and provides the strength and wisdom needed to follow Him. By making prayer a regular part of our routine, we can deepen our relationship with God and receive the support needed to live a life of distinction.

To not be conformed to this world, we must also be committed to sharing the gospel and making disciples. This means being willing to speak about our faith and to invest in the spiritual growth of others. By prioritizing evangelism and discipleship, we demonstrate our commitment to following Jesus' command to make disciples of all nations. This dedication to sharing the gospel helps to ensure that our lives are focused on advancing God's kingdom and reflecting His character.

Resisting conformity to the world requires us to be committed to living out our faith in practical ways. This involves demonstrating our commitment to God through our actions, such as showing love, kindness, and compassion to others. By living out our faith, we can make a positive impact and provide a powerful witness to those around us. This practical expression of our faith helps to ensure that our lives reflect the principles of distinction.

In conclusion, "Do not be conformed to this world" is a powerful command that emphasizes distinction. Romans 12:2 urges believers to resist the pressures and influences of the world and to seek transformation through the renewal of their minds. Distinction involves understanding the difference between the world's values and God's values, cultivating a renewed mind, developing strong convictions, being vigilant about influences, pursuing spiritual growth, taking a stand for our faith, making choices that honor God, cultivating humility and dependence, practicing spiritual disciplines, serving others, being grateful, making sacrifices, being patient and persistent, seeking to be peacemakers, being honest and trustworthy, committing to continuous learning, being creative and innovative, building strong relationships, being generous, practicing forgiveness, being flexible, committing to prayer, sharing the gospel, and living out our faith practically. By embracing this command, we can ensure that our lives reflect our commitment to living a life that is distinct from the world and honors God. In conclusion, "Do not be conformed to this world" is a command that calls for distinction, encouraging us to live a life that reflects God's character and demonstrates His good and perfect will.

Chapter 12 - Declare "Declare his glory among the heathen"

Psalm 96:3 - "Declare his glory among the heathen, his wonders among all people."

This verse emphasizes the importance of declaring, urging believers to share the glory and wonders of God with those who do not know Him. To declare his glory means to openly and boldly proclaim the greatness, majesty, and deeds of God to everyone, especially to those who are not part of the faith. Declaration in this context refers to the intentional and enthusiastic act of spreading the message of God's goodness, power, and love to all people. This command encourages us to be vocal about our faith, to share our experiences of God's work in our lives, and to make known the incredible things He has done, so that others might come to know and worship Him.

Declaring God's glory begins with a deep understanding and appreciation of who God is and what He has done. This involves spending time in prayer, reading the Bible, and reflecting on the many ways God has shown His power and love throughout history and in our personal lives. By cultivating a heart of gratitude and awe for God's works, we can speak authentically and passionately about His glory. This personal relationship with God fuels our desire to share His greatness with others and helps us to articulate our faith with conviction.

To declare God's glory, we must also recognize the importance of sharing our faith with those who do not know God. This means being intentional about reaching out to people from all walks of life, including those who may have different beliefs or no beliefs at all. By being inclusive in our declaration, we fulfill the call to make God's wonders known among all people. This inclusivity demonstrates God's love for everyone and His desire for all to come to know Him.

Declaring God's glory requires us to be bold and confident in our faith. This means overcoming fear and hesitation, and being willing to speak about God even when it may be uncomfortable or challenging. Boldness in declaring God's glory comes from a deep trust in His power and a commitment to His command to spread the gospel. By stepping out in faith, we can share the message of God's greatness with courage and enthusiasm, inspiring others to listen and respond.

To declare God's glory, we must also be prepared to share our personal testimonies of His work in our lives. Testimonies are powerful tools for witnessing because they provide tangible evidence of God's presence and action. By sharing how God has transformed our lives, answered our prayers, and provided for our needs, we can help others see the reality of His glory and be encouraged to seek Him for themselves. Personal stories of faith make the abstract concepts of God's greatness and love more relatable and impactful. Declaring God's glory involves using our talents and gifts to spread His message. Whether through speaking, writing, music, art, or other forms of expression, we can creatively and effectively communicate the wonders of God. By using our unique abilities to declare His glory, we can reach a diverse audience and make a lasting impact. This creative approach allows us to connect with people in meaningful ways and to share the message of God's greatness in a variety of contexts.

To declare God's glory, we must also be knowledgeable about the Bible and its teachings. Understanding Scripture helps us to accurately and effectively communicate the truths about God's character and works. By studying the Bible and seeking to grow in our knowledge of God, we can be better equipped to share His message with others. This biblical foundation provides the basis for our declaration and ensures that we are sharing the authentic and powerful message of God's glory.

Declaring God's glory requires us to be persistent and consistent in our efforts. Sharing our faith is not a one-time event, but an ongoing commitment to making God's greatness known. By continually looking for opportunities to speak about God and to demonstrate His love through our actions, we can make a sustained impact. This persistence shows our dedication to fulfilling God's command and our desire to see His glory proclaimed among all people.

To declare God's glory, we must also live lives that reflect His character. Our actions and attitudes should demonstrate the love, kindness, and righteousness of God. By living in a way that honors God, we provide a powerful testimony to His transforming power. Our lives become a living declaration of His glory, attracting others to seek the source of our faith and joy. This alignment between our words and actions reinforces the message we proclaim and adds credibility to our witness.

Declaring God's glory involves being empathetic and understanding towards those we are trying to reach. This means listening to their stories, understanding their perspectives, and addressing their questions and doubts with compassion and respect. By building genuine relationships and showing that we care, we can create an environment where people feel valued and open to hearing about God's glory. Empathy helps to bridge the gap between different beliefs and experiences, making our declaration more effective and impactful.

To declare God's glory, we must also pray for opportunities and guidance. Prayer is essential in seeking God's direction and empowerment for our efforts. By praying for boldness, wisdom, and open hearts, we can be better prepared to share God's message and to respond to the needs of those we encounter. Prayer also helps us to stay connected to God's will and to rely on His strength rather than our own. This dependence on God ensures that our declaration is led by the Holy Spirit and aligned with His purposes.Declaring God's glory requires us to be patient and understanding. Sharing our faith can be met with resistance or indifference, and it is important to remain patient and persistent. By showing patience, we demonstrate the love and grace of God, allowing others to come to faith in their own time.

This patience also helps us to build trust and credibility, making our message more impactful over time.

To declare God's glory, we must also be adaptable and flexible in our approach. Different people respond to different methods of communication, and it is important to be willing to adjust our approach to meet their needs. By being flexible, we can find the most effective ways to share God's message and to reach a diverse audience. This adaptability ensures that our declaration is relevant and accessible to everyone.

Declaring God's glory involves being authentic and genuine in our interactions. People are more likely to respond to a message that is delivered with sincerity and honesty. By being authentic, we can build trust and credibility, making our declaration more impactful. Authenticity also helps us to connect with others on a deeper level, allowing us to share the message of God's glory in a meaningful and personal way.

To declare God's glory, we must also be committed to personal growth and spiritual development. This involves continually seeking to deepen our relationship with God and to grow in our understanding of His Word. By pursuing spiritual growth, we can be better equipped to share God's message and to live lives that reflect His glory. This commitment to growth ensures that our declaration is rooted in a strong and vibrant faith.

Declaring God's glory requires us to be respectful and considerate of others' beliefs and experiences. This means engaging in conversations with humility and respect, recognizing that everyone is on their own spiritual journey. By showing respect, we create a safe and open environment where people feel valued and heard. This respect helps to build trust and credibility, making our declaration more effective.

To declare God's glory, we must also be enthusiastic and passionate about our faith. Enthusiasm is contagious, and it can inspire others to seek the joy and fulfillment that we have found in God. By sharing our faith with passion and excitement, we can draw others to the message of God's glory. This enthusiasm also helps to sustain our own commitment to declaring God's greatness, keeping us motivated and energized.

Declaring God's glory involves being humble and willing to learn from others. This means being open to feedback and willing to adjust our approach based on what we learn. By showing humility, we demonstrate that we are not just trying to impose our beliefs on others, but that we genuinely care about their spiritual journey. This humility helps to build trust and credibility, making our declaration more effective.

To declare God's glory, we must also be consistent in our message and actions. Consistency builds trust and credibility, showing that our faith is not just a passing interest but a deeply held conviction. By being consistent, we reinforce the message of God's glory and demonstrate the authenticity of our faith. This consistency helps to make our declaration more impactful and meaningful.

Declaring God's glory requires us to be compassionate and loving in our interactions. This means showing genuine care and concern for others and being willing to help and support them in their journey. By demonstrating compassion, we reflect the love of God and make our declaration more relatable and impactful. This compassion helps to create an environment where people feel valued and open to hearing about God's glory.

To declare God's glory, we must also be persistent and committed. Sharing our faith can be challenging, and it is important to remain steadfast in our efforts. By showing persistence, we demonstrate our dedication to fulfilling God's command and our desire to see His glory proclaimed among all people. This persistence helps to ensure that our declaration is sustained and effective.

Declaring God's glory involves being creative and innovative in our approach. This means finding new and effective ways to share God's message and to reach a diverse audience. By being creative, we can make our declaration more engaging and impactful. Creativity allows us to connect with people in meaningful ways and to share the message of God's greatness in a variety of contexts.

To declare God's glory, we must also be committed to building strong and supportive relationships with other believers. Fellowship with other Christians provides encouragement, accountability, and support in our efforts to declare God's glory. By sharing our experiences and challenges with others, we can grow together and strengthen our resolve to make God's greatness known. Strong relationships help to create a sense of community and belonging, which are essential for effective declaration.

Declaring God's glory requires us to be generous with our time, resources, and talents. Generosity reflects God's character and demonstrates our commitment to living according to His principles. By being willing to share what we have with others, we can make a positive impact and show the love of Christ in practical ways. Generosity helps to counteract the materialism and selfishness that characterize the world, setting us apart as followers of Jesus.

To declare God's glory, we must also be committed to practicing forgiveness and reconciliation. This means being willing to let go of grudges and to seek healing in our relationships. Forgiveness is a powerful act of distinction, as it reflects God's grace and mercy. By practicing forgiveness, we can create an environment of love and compassion, which helps to distinguish us from the world.

Declaring God's glory involves being flexible and adaptable in our faith journey. This means being open to new experiences and willing to adjust our approaches as needed. Flexibility allows us to respond effectively to the challenges we face and to remain resilient in our commitment to living a life that honors God. By being adaptable, we can stay focused on our goal of distinction, even in the face of changing circumstances.

Living a life of distinction involves being committed to prayer and seeking God's guidance in all aspects of our lives. Prayer is a vital aspect of resisting conformity to the world, as it connects us to God's presence and provides the strength and wisdom needed to follow Him. By making prayer a regular part of our routine, we can deepen our relationship with God and receive the support needed to live a life of distinction.

To declare God's glory, we must also be committed to sharing the gospel and making disciples. This means being willing to speak about our faith and to invest in the spiritual growth of others. By prioritizing evangelism and discipleship, we demonstrate our commitment to following Jesus' command to make disciples of all nations. This dedication to sharing the gospel helps to ensure that our lives are focused on advancing God's kingdom and reflecting His character.

Declaring God's glory requires us to be committed to living out our faith in practical ways. This involves demonstrating our commitment to God through our actions, such as showing love, kindness, and compassion to others. By living out our faith, we can make a positive impact and provide a powerful witness to those around us. This practical expression of our faith helps to ensure that our lives reflect the principles of distinction. In conclusion, "Declare his glory among the heathen" is a powerful command that emphasizes declaration. Psalm 96:3 urges believers to share the glory and wonders of God with those who do not know Him. Declaration involves understanding and appreciating who God is, recognizing the importance of sharing our faith, being bold and confident, sharing personal testimonies, using our talents, being knowledgeable about the Bible, being persistent, living lives that reflect God's character, being empathetic, praying for opportunities and guidance, being patient, being adaptable, being authentic, committing to personal growth, being respectful, being enthusiastic, being humble, being consistent, being compassionate, being creative, building strong relationships, being generous, practicing forgiveness, being flexible, committing to prayer, sharing the gospel, and living out our faith practically. By embracing this command, we can ensure that our lives reflect our commitment to declaring God's glory and making His wonders known among all people. In conclusion, "Declare his glory among the heathen" is a command that calls for declaration, encouraging us to share the greatness, majesty, and deeds of God with everyone, especially those who do not know Him.

Chapter 13 – Duty - "Do justly, love mercy, walk humbly"

Micah 6:8 - "He hath shewed thee, O man, what is good; and what doth the LORD require of thee, but to do justly, and to love mercy, and to walk humbly with thy God?"

This verse emphasizes duty, urging believers to live lives characterized by justice, mercy, and humility. To do justly means to act with fairness and integrity in all our dealings. To love mercy means to show compassion and kindness to others. To walk humbly with God means to live in a way that recognizes our dependence on Him and seeks to honor Him in all we do. This command encourages us to live out these principles daily, demonstrating our commitment to God's values and reflecting His character in our actions and attitudes.

Doing justly involves treating others with fairness and respect, ensuring that our actions are guided by a sense of justice. This means being honest in our dealings, avoiding deceit and manipulation, and standing up for what is right, even when it is difficult. By committing to justice, we create an environment of trust and respect, where everyone is treated with dignity and fairness. This commitment to justice is a reflection of God's own character, as He is a God of justice who desires that His people act with integrity.

To do justly, we must also be willing to speak out against injustice and to advocate for those who are marginalized and oppressed. This means using our voice and influence to bring attention to issues of injustice and to work towards creating a more equitable society. By standing up for justice, we demonstrate our commitment to living according to God's values and to making a positive impact in the world. This advocacy helps to create a society where justice prevails and where everyone has the opportunity to thrive.

Loving mercy involves showing compassion and kindness to others, recognizing that we have all experienced God's mercy in our own lives. This means being willing to forgive those who have wronged us, to offer help to those in need, and to treat others with kindness and understanding. By loving mercy, we reflect the heart of God, who is merciful and compassionate towards us. This love for mercy helps to create a culture of empathy and support, where people feel valued and cared for.

To love mercy, we must also be willing to go out of our way to help others, even when it is inconvenient or challenging. This means looking for opportunities to serve and support those around us, whether through acts of kindness, words of encouragement, or practical assistance. By demonstrating mercy in our actions, we show the love of God to those around us and create a ripple effect of kindness and compassion. This commitment to mercy helps to build strong and supportive communities, where everyone feels valued and cared for. Walking humbly with God involves recognizing our dependence on Him and seeking to live in a way that honors Him. This means acknowledging that we are not self-sufficient, but that we rely on God's guidance, strength, and provision. By walking humbly with God, we cultivate a spirit of humility, which allows us to submit to His will and to seek His direction in all aspects of our lives. This humility helps us to stay grounded in our faith and to avoid the pitfalls of pride and self-reliance.

To walk humbly with God, we must also be willing to listen to His voice and to follow His leading. This means spending time in prayer, reading the Bible, and seeking the guidance of the Holy Spirit. By staying connected to God through these spiritual practices, we can discern His will and make decisions that align with His purposes. This commitment to walking humbly with God helps us to stay focused on our faith and to live in a way that honors Him.

Doing justly, loving mercy, and walking humbly with God requires a daily commitment to living out these principles in our lives. This means being intentional about our actions and attitudes, seeking to reflect God's character in everything we do. By making these principles a priority, we can create a positive impact in our communities and demonstrate our commitment to God's values. This daily commitment helps to ensure that our lives are a reflection of God's love and grace.

To do justly, love mercy, and walk humbly with God, we must also be willing to examine our own hearts and to seek God's help in areas where we fall short. This means being open to conviction and correction, allowing God to shape and refine our character. By being honest about our weaknesses and seeking God's help, we can grow in our ability to live out these principles. This willingness to be transformed by God helps to ensure that our lives are continually growing in alignment with His will.

Doing justly, loving mercy, and walking humbly with God involves being part of a supportive community of believers. Fellowship with other Christians provides encouragement, accountability, and support in our efforts to live out these principles. By sharing our experiences and challenges with others, we can grow together and strengthen our commitment to justice, mercy, and humility. This sense of community helps to create an environment where God's values are lived out and where everyone is encouraged to grow in their faith.

To do justly, love mercy, and walk humbly with God, we must also be committed to personal growth and spiritual development. This involves continually seeking to deepen our understanding of God's Word, to grow in our relationship with Him, and to develop our spiritual disciplines. By pursuing spiritual growth, we can strengthen our commitment to living out these principles and enhance our ability to reflect God's character. This dedication to growth helps to ensure that our faith remains dynamic and alive.

Doing justly, loving mercy, and walking humbly with God requires us to be intentional about our actions and decisions. This means making choices that reflect God's values and seeking to live in a way that honors Him. By being intentional, we can ensure that our lives are a reflection of God's love and grace. This intentionality helps to create a positive impact in our communities and to demonstrate our commitment to God's principles.

To do justly, love mercy, and walk humbly with God, we must also be willing to make sacrifices for the sake of our faith. This means being prepared to give up certain comforts, conveniences, or opportunities that conflict with our commitment to God. Sacrifice is a key aspect of living out these principles, as it demonstrates our willingness to prioritize God's will above our own desires. By making sacrifices, we show that our faith is more important than worldly gain, and we strengthen our resolve to live according to God's principles.

Doing justly, loving mercy, and walking humbly with God involves being patient and persistent in our efforts. Living out these principles is a lifelong journey that requires dedication and perseverance. By being patient and persistent, we can continue to make a positive impact and to uphold our commitment to justice, mercy, and humility. This persistence helps to ensure that our lives are a reflection of God's values and that we remain steadfast in our faith.

To do justly, love mercy, and walk humbly with God, we must also be willing to seek justice and to stand up for what is right. This means being willing to speak out against injustice and to take action to promote fairness and equality. By prioritizing justice, we demonstrate our commitment to living according to God's values and to making a positive impact in the world. This dedication to justice helps to ensure that our lives reflect the principles of God's kingdom. Doing justly, loving mercy, and walking humbly with God requires us to be compassionate and loving in our interactions. This means showing genuine care and concern for others and being willing to help and support them in their journey. By demonstrating compassion, we reflect the love of God and make our declaration more relatable and impactful. This compassion helps to create an environment where people feel valued and open to hearing about God's glory.

To do justly, love mercy, and walk humbly with God, we must also be committed to forgiveness and reconciliation. This means being willing to let go of grudges and to seek healing in our relationships. Forgiveness is a powerful act of distinction, as it reflects God's grace and mercy. By practicing forgiveness, we can create an environment of love and compassion, which helps to distinguish us from the world.

Doing justly, loving mercy, and walking humbly with God involves being flexible and adaptable in our faith journey. This means being open to new experiences and willing to adjust our approaches as needed. Flexibility allows us to respond effectively to the challenges we face and to remain resilient in our commitment to living a life that honors God. By being adaptable, we can stay focused on our goal of distinction, even in the face of changing circumstances.

Living a life of distinction involves being committed to prayer and seeking God's guidance in all aspects of our lives. Prayer is a vital aspect of resisting conformity to the world, as it connects us to God's presence and provides the strength and wisdom needed to follow Him. By making prayer a regular part of our routine, we can deepen our relationship with God and receive the support needed to live a life of distinction.

To do justly, love mercy, and walk humbly with God, we must also be committed to sharing the gospel and making disciples. This means being willing to speak about our faith and to invest in the spiritual growth of others. By prioritizing evangelism and discipleship, we demonstrate our commitment to following Jesus' command to make disciples of all nations. This dedication to sharing the gospel helps to ensure that our lives are focused on advancing God's kingdom and reflecting His character.

Doing justly, loving mercy, and walking humbly with God requires us to be committed to living out our faith in practical ways. This involves demonstrating our commitment to God through our actions, such as showing love, kindness, and compassion to others. By living out our faith, we can make a positive impact and provide a powerful witness to those around us. This practical expression of our faith helps to ensure that our lives reflect the principles of distinction.

In conclusion, "Do justly, love mercy, walk humbly" is a powerful command that emphasizes duty. Micah 6:8 urges believers to live lives characterized by justice, mercy, and humility. Duty involves understanding and appreciating who God is, recognizing the importance of sharing our faith, being bold and confident, sharing personal testimonies, using our talents, being knowledgeable about the Bible, being persistent, living lives that reflect God's character, being empathetic, praying for opportunities and guidance, being patient, being adaptable, being authentic, committing to personal growth, being respectful, being enthusiastic, being humble, being consistent, being compassionate, being creative, building strong relationships, being generous, practicing forgiveness, being flexible, committing to prayer, sharing the gospel, and living out our faith practically. By embracing this command, we can ensure that our lives reflect our commitment to doing justly, loving mercy, and walking humbly with God. In conclusion, "Do justly, love mercy, walk humbly" is a command that calls for duty, encouraging us to live a life that reflects God's character and demonstrates His good and perfect will.

Chapter 14 - Draw - "Draw near with a true heart"

Hebrews 10:22 - "Let us draw near with a true heart in full assurance of faith, having our hearts sprinkled from an evil conscience, and our bodies washed with pure water."
This verse emphasizes the act of drawing near to God with sincerity and authenticity, urging believers to approach God with genuine faith and a clean conscience. To draw near with a true heart means to come before God with honesty, transparency, and a deep sense of trust in His grace and mercy. Drawing near in this context refers to the intentional effort to deepen our relationship with God, seeking His presence, and living in a way that reflects our commitment to Him. This command encourages us to embrace a lifestyle of sincerity, faith, and purity, demonstrating our devotion to God through our actions, thoughts, and attitudes.

Drawing near with a true heart begins with cultivating a sincere desire to know and experience God more deeply. This involves setting aside time each day to pray, read the Bible, and meditate on His Word. By making these practices a regular part of our routine, we can cultivate a habit of seeking God and growing closer to Him. This daily commitment helps to center our lives around God and to prioritize our relationship with Him above all else. As we draw near to God with a true heart, we open ourselves to experiencing His love, grace, and guidance in new and profound ways.

To draw near with a true heart, we must also be willing to examine our own hearts and to seek God's help in areas where we fall short. This means being honest about our weaknesses, sins, and struggles, and asking God to cleanse and purify our hearts. By allowing God to reveal and address the areas of our lives that need transformation, we can develop a deeper sense of authenticity and sincerity in our relationship with Him. This willingness to be vulnerable before God helps to foster a genuine and transparent relationship, free from pretense and hypocrisy.

Drawing near with a true heart requires us to approach God with full assurance of faith. This means trusting in God's promises and believing that He is faithful and just to forgive our sins and to cleanse us from all unrighteousness. By having confidence in God's grace and mercy, we can draw near to Him without fear or hesitation, knowing that He welcomes us with open arms. This assurance of faith helps to strengthen our relationship with God and to build a foundation of trust and security in His love.

To draw near with a true heart, we must also be committed to living a life of purity and holiness. This involves seeking to align our thoughts, actions, and attitudes with God's will and striving to live according to His standards. By pursuing holiness, we demonstrate our desire to honor God and to reflect His character in our lives. This commitment to purity helps to create a clean and honest heart, allowing us to draw near to God with sincerity and integrity. As we strive to live a life that is pleasing to God, we can experience the fullness of His presence and the joy of walking in His ways.

Drawing near with a true heart involves being open to the work of the Holy Spirit in our lives. The Holy Spirit provides guidance, comfort, and strength as we seek to follow God and to live according to His will. By being sensitive to the Spirit's leading and allowing Him to transform our hearts and minds, we can draw closer to God and experience His presence in new and powerful ways. This openness to the Holy Spirit helps to ensure that our relationship with God is dynamic and alive, continually growing and deepening.

To draw near with a true heart, we must also be willing to let go of anything that hinders our relationship with God. This includes letting go of sinful behaviors, unhealthy relationships, and distractions that pull us away from God. By surrendering these things to God and seeking His help to overcome them, we can create space in our lives for His presence and work. This surrender helps to purify our hearts and to draw us closer to God in our daily walk. As we let go of the things that hold us back, we can experience the freedom and joy that come from living fully in God's presence.

Drawing near with a true heart requires us to be humble and to recognize our dependence on God. This means acknowledging that we cannot navigate life on our own and that we need God's guidance, strength, and provision. By humbling ourselves before God and seeking His help, we open ourselves to His grace and support. This humility allows us to draw near to God with a true heart, free from pride and self-reliance. As we depend on God and trust in His goodness, we can experience the peace and security that come from knowing that He is in control.

To draw near with a true heart, we must also cultivate a heart of gratitude and thankfulness. This involves recognizing the many ways that God has blessed us and expressing our gratitude through praise and worship. By focusing on God's goodness and faithfulness, we can develop a heart of gratitude that enhances our joy and contentment in Him. This gratitude helps to keep our hearts aligned with God's will and to remind us of His constant presence and provision. As we cultivate a thankful heart, we can draw near to God with a true heart, filled with appreciation and love for all that He has done.

Drawing near with a true heart involves being part of a supportive community of believers. Fellowship with other Christians provides encouragement, accountability, and support in our spiritual journey. By sharing our experiences, challenges, and victories with others, we can grow together in our relationship with God. This sense of community helps to strengthen our faith and to draw us closer to God as we support and uplift one another. Being part of a faith community provides a powerful source of encouragement and inspiration, helping us to stay committed to drawing near to God with a true heart.

To draw near with a true heart, we must also be committed to personal growth and spiritual development. This involves continually seeking to deepen our understanding of God's Word, to grow in our relationship with Him, and to develop our spiritual disciplines. By pursuing spiritual growth, we can strengthen our commitment to drawing near to God and to living a life that reflects His character. This dedication to growth helps to ensure that our faith remains dynamic and alive, continually deepening our connection with God.

Drawing near with a true heart requires us to be intentional about our actions and decisions. This means making choices that reflect our commitment to God and seeking to live in a way that honors Him. By being intentional, we can ensure that our lives are a reflection of God's love and grace. This intentionality helps to create a positive impact in our communities and to demonstrate our commitment to God's principles. As we make intentional choices that align with God's will, we can draw near to Him with a true heart, fully dedicated to His purposes.

To draw near with a true heart, we must also be willing to make sacrifices for the sake of our faith. This means being prepared to give up certain comforts, conveniences, or opportunities that conflict with our commitment to God. Sacrifice is a key aspect of drawing near to God, as it demonstrates our willingness to prioritize His will above our own desires. By making sacrifices, we show that our faith is more important than worldly gain, and we strengthen our resolve to live according to God's principles. As we make sacrifices for our faith, we can draw near to God with a true heart, fully devoted to Him.

Drawing near with a true heart involves being patient and persistent in our efforts. Developing a deep and meaningful relationship with God takes time and effort, and it requires us to remain steadfast in our commitment. By being patient and persistent, we can overcome the obstacles and distractions that seek to pull us away from God. This perseverance helps to strengthen our faith and to deepen our relationship with Him. As we remain patient and persistent in our pursuit of God, we can draw near to Him with a true heart, fully dedicated to our spiritual journey.

To draw near with a true heart, we must also be open to the guidance and direction of the Holy Spirit. The Holy Spirit provides the wisdom and strength we need to navigate life's challenges and to stay focused on our faith. By being sensitive to the Spirit's leading, we can receive the support and encouragement needed to stay on the path of discipleship. This openness to the Holy Spirit helps to ensure that our relationship with God is continually growing and deepening, allowing us to draw near to Him with a true heart.

Drawing near with a true heart requires us to be grateful for the blessings and opportunities that God has given us. Gratitude helps us to maintain a positive and joyful attitude, even in the face of challenges and difficulties. By focusing on the goodness of God and expressing thankfulness, we can stay motivated and encouraged in our journey of faith. This gratitude helps to keep our hearts centered on God and to remind us of His constant presence and provision. As we cultivate a thankful heart, we can draw near to God with a true heart, filled with appreciation and love for all that He has done.

To draw near with a true heart, we must also be willing to invest in the well-being of others. This means using our time, resources, and talents to serve and support those around us. By prioritizing the needs of others, we demonstrate the love of Jesus and fulfill His command to love our neighbor as ourselves. This commitment to serving others helps to cultivate a spirit of generosity and compassion, which are essential aspects of drawing near to God with a true heart. As we invest in the well-being of others, we can draw near to God with a true heart, fully dedicated to His purposes.

Drawing near with a true heart requires us to be honest and transparent in our relationships. This means being truthful in our words and actions and being willing to admit our mistakes and seek forgiveness. By practicing honesty, we build trust and credibility in our relationships, reflecting the integrity of Jesus. This commitment to truth helps to ensure that our interactions with others are genuine and authentic, allowing us to draw near to God with a true heart.

To draw near with a true heart, we must also be willing to seek justice and to stand up for what is right. This means being willing to speak out against injustice and to take action to promote fairness and equality. By prioritizing justice, we demonstrate our commitment to living according to God's values and to making a positive impact in the world. This dedication to justice helps to ensure that our lives reflect the principles of God's kingdom, allowing us to draw near to Him with a true heart.

Drawing near with a true heart involves being mindful of our physical and emotional well-being. Taking care of our bodies and minds by getting enough rest, eating well, and seeking support when needed helps us to better manage the demands of following Jesus. By prioritizing self-care, we can ensure that we have the energy and resilience needed to continue our journey of drawing near to God. This mindfulness helps to sustain our commitment to following Jesus and to living a life that honors Him.

To draw near with a true heart, we must also be willing to seek wisdom and guidance from others. This means being open to learning from the experiences and insights of mature believers. By seeking counsel and mentorship, we can gain valuable support and encouragement in our journey of drawing near to God. This openness to guidance helps to ensure that we are growing and maturing in our faith, allowing us to draw near to God with a true heart.

Drawing near with a true heart requires a commitment to living out our faith in practical ways. This involves demonstrating our commitment to God through our actions, such as showing love, kindness, and compassion to others. By living out our faith, we can make a positive impact and provide a powerful witness to those around us. This practical expression of our faith helps to ensure that our lives reflect the principles of drawing near to God with a true heart.

In conclusion, "Draw near with a true heart" is a powerful command that emphasizes drawing near. Hebrews 10:22 urges believers to approach God with sincerity and authenticity, to cultivate a genuine faith, and to live with a clean conscience. Drawing near involves understanding and appreciating who God is, examining our hearts, trusting in God's promises, living a life of purity, being open to the Holy Spirit, letting go of hindrances, cultivating humility, expressing gratitude, being part of a supportive community, pursuing personal growth, being intentional in our actions, making sacrifices, being patient and persistent, seeking guidance, investing in others, practicing honesty, seeking justice, prioritizing self-care, seeking wisdom, and living out our faith practically. By embracing this command, we can ensure that our lives reflect our commitment to drawing near to God with a true heart and experiencing the fullness of His presence. In conclusion, "Draw near with a true heart" is a command that calls for drawing near, encouraging us to seek a close and intimate relationship with God and to experience the joy and fulfillment that come from knowing and loving Him.

Chapter 15 – Departure - "Depart from iniquity"

2 Timothy 2:19 - "Nevertheless the foundation of God standeth sure, having this seal, The Lord knoweth them that are his. And, Let every one that nameth the name of Christ depart from iniquity."

This verse emphasizes departure, urging believers to turn away from sinful behaviors and to live lives that reflect their commitment to Christ. To depart from iniquity means to reject and avoid actions, thoughts, and attitudes that are contrary to God's will. Departure in this context refers to the deliberate and conscious decision to separate oneself from sin and to pursue a life of righteousness. This command encourages us to embrace a lifestyle of holiness, demonstrating our devotion to God through our choices and actions.

Departing from iniquity begins with a clear understanding of what iniquity is. Iniquity refers to sinful behaviors, actions, and attitudes that go against God's commands and principles. This includes lying, stealing, cheating, hatred, jealousy, and any other actions that harm others or ourselves. By recognizing what constitutes iniquity, we can be more vigilant in identifying and avoiding such behaviors in our lives. This awareness is the first step in the process of departing from iniquity, as it helps us to see the areas where we need to make changes.

To depart from iniquity, we must cultivate a heart of repentance. Repentance involves feeling genuine sorrow for our sins, confessing them to God, and turning away from them. By acknowledging our sins and seeking God's forgiveness, we can experience His grace and mercy, which empower us to live differently. This process of repentance is essential for departing from iniquity, as it allows us to start fresh and to commit to a new way of living. By continually practicing repentance, we can stay on the path of righteousness and avoid falling back into sinful patterns. Departing from iniquity requires us to be intentional about our actions and decisions. This means making choices that align with God's will and avoiding situations that may lead us into temptation. By being intentional, we can create a life that reflects our commitment to holiness and righteousness. This intentionality helps to ensure that our actions and attitudes are consistent with our faith, allowing us to depart from iniquity effectively. As we make deliberate choices to follow God's commands, we can experience the freedom and joy that come from living a life that honors Him.

To depart from iniquity, we must also seek the guidance and strength of the Holy Spirit. The Holy Spirit provides the power and wisdom we need to overcome sin and to live according to God's will. By relying on the Holy Spirit, we can resist temptation and stay strong in our commitment to righteousness. This dependence on the Holy Spirit helps to ensure that our efforts to depart from iniquity are supported by God's strength, rather than our own. As we seek the Holy Spirit's guidance, we can navigate life's challenges with confidence and faith. Departing from iniquity involves surrounding ourselves with positive influences. This means seeking out relationships with other believers who encourage and support our commitment to holiness. By being part of a community of faith, we can receive the accountability and encouragement we need to stay on the path of righteousness. This community helps to reinforce our commitment to departing from iniquity and provides a source of strength and support. As we surround ourselves with positive influences, we can stay focused on our goal of living a life that honors God.

To depart from iniquity, we must also immerse ourselves in God's Word. The Bible provides the guidance and instruction we need to understand God's will and to live according to His principles. By studying Scripture regularly, we can gain a deeper understanding of what it means to live a holy life and to avoid sin. This engagement with God's Word helps to equip us with the knowledge and wisdom we need to depart from iniquity. As we immerse ourselves in Scripture, we can strengthen our faith and stay grounded in God's truth.

Departing from iniquity requires us to be humble and willing to accept correction. This means being open to feedback and willing to make changes when necessary. By being humble, we can recognize our own shortcomings and seek God's help to overcome them. This willingness to accept correction is essential for departing from iniquity, as it allows us to grow and improve in our walk with God. As we embrace humility, we can stay teachable and responsive to God's guidance.

To depart from iniquity, we must also develop self-discipline. Self-discipline involves controlling our desires and impulses and making choices that reflect our commitment to holiness. By practicing self-discipline, we can resist temptation and stay focused on our goal of living a life that honors God. This discipline helps to ensure that our actions and attitudes are consistent with our faith, allowing us to depart from iniquity effectively. As we develop self-discipline, we can experience the peace and satisfaction that come from living according to God's will.

Departing from iniquity involves being proactive in addressing areas of weakness. This means identifying the aspects of our lives where we are most susceptible to temptation and taking steps to strengthen our defenses. By being proactive, we can avoid falling into sinful patterns and stay committed to righteousness. This proactive approach helps to ensure that we are continually growing and improving in our walk with God. As we address areas of weakness, we can strengthen our resolve to depart from iniquity and live a life that honors God.

To depart from iniquity, we must also cultivate a heart of gratitude. Gratitude helps us to focus on the blessings and opportunities that God has given us, rather than on the temptations and distractions of the world. By developing a heart of gratitude, we can stay motivated and encouraged in our efforts to live a holy life. This gratitude helps to keep our hearts aligned with God's will and to remind us of His constant presence and provision. As we cultivate gratitude, we can depart from iniquity with a joyful and thankful heart.

Departing from iniquity requires us to seek God's guidance in all aspects of our lives. This means praying for wisdom and discernment in our decisions and being open to His leading. By seeking God's guidance, we can make choices that reflect His will and avoid the pitfalls of sin. This dependence on God's guidance helps to ensure that our efforts to depart from iniquity are supported by His wisdom and strength. As we seek God's direction, we can navigate life's challenges with confidence and faith.

To depart from iniquity, we must also be committed to personal growth and spiritual development. This involves continually seeking to deepen our understanding of God's Word, to grow in our relationship with Him, and to develop our spiritual disciplines. By pursuing spiritual growth, we can strengthen our commitment to departing from iniquity and enhance our ability to live according to God's will. This dedication to growth helps to ensure that our faith remains dynamic and alive, continually deepening our connection with God.

Departing from iniquity involves being intentional about our relationships. This means seeking out friendships and connections that support our commitment to holiness and avoiding those that may lead us into temptation. By being intentional about our relationships, we can create a supportive environment that encourages us to live according to God's will. This intentionality helps to ensure that our actions and attitudes are consistent with our faith, allowing us to depart from iniquity effectively. As we build positive relationships, we can stay focused on our goal of living a life that honors God.

To depart from iniquity, we must also be willing to make sacrifices for the sake of our faith. This means being prepared to give up certain comforts, conveniences, or opportunities that conflict with our commitment to God. Sacrifice is a key aspect of departing from iniquity, as it demonstrates our willingness to prioritize God's will above our own desires. By making sacrifices, we show that our faith is more important than worldly gain, and we strengthen our resolve to live according to God's principles. As we make sacrifices for our faith, we can depart from iniquity with a committed and dedicated heart.

Departing from iniquity requires us to be patient and persistent in our efforts. Overcoming sin and living a holy life is a lifelong journey that requires dedication and perseverance. By being patient and persistent, we can continue to make progress and to uphold our commitment to righteousness. This persistence helps to ensure that our lives are a reflection of God's values and that we remain steadfast in our faith. As we remain patient and persistent in our pursuit of holiness, we can depart from iniquity with a determined and unwavering heart.

To depart from iniquity, we must also be open to the work of the Holy Spirit in our lives. The Holy Spirit provides the power and guidance we need to overcome sin and to live according to God's will. By being sensitive to the Spirit's leading and allowing Him to transform our hearts and minds, we can depart from iniquity and live a life that honors God. This openness to the Holy Spirit helps to ensure that our efforts to depart from iniquity are supported by God's strength, rather than our own. As we seek the Holy Spirit's guidance, we can navigate life's challenges with confidence and faith.

Departing from iniquity involves being grateful for the blessings and opportunities that God has given us. Gratitude helps us to maintain a positive and joyful attitude, even in the face of challenges and difficulties. By focusing on the goodness of God and expressing thankfulness, we can stay motivated and encouraged in our journey of faith. This gratitude helps to keep our hearts centered on God and to remind us of His constant presence and provision. As we cultivate a thankful heart, we can depart from iniquity with a joyful and appreciative spirit.

To depart from iniquity, we must also be willing to invest in the well-being of others. This means using our time, resources, and talents to serve and support those around us. By prioritizing the needs of others, we demonstrate the love of Jesus and fulfill His command to love our neighbor as ourselves. This commitment to serving others helps to cultivate a spirit

of generosity and compassion, which are essential aspects of departing from iniquity. As we invest in the well-being of others, we can depart from iniquity with a selfless and compassionate heart.

Departing from iniquity requires us to be honest and transparent in our relationships. This means being truthful in our words and actions and being willing to admit our mistakes and seek forgiveness. By practicing honesty, we build trust and credibility in our relationships, reflecting the integrity of Jesus. This commitment to truth helps to ensure that our interactions with others are genuine and authentic, allowing us to depart from iniquity effectively. As we embrace honesty, we can depart from iniquity with a sincere and truthful heart.

To depart from iniquity, we must also be willing to seek justice and to stand up for what is right. This means being willing to speak out against injustice and to take action to promote fairness and equality. By prioritizing justice, we demonstrate our commitment to living according to God's values and to making a positive impact in the world. This dedication to justice helps to ensure that our lives reflect the principles of God's kingdom, allowing us to depart from iniquity with a righteous and just heart.

Departing from iniquity involves being mindful of our physical and emotional well-being. Taking care of our bodies and minds by getting enough rest, eating well, and seeking support when needed helps us to better manage the demands of following Jesus. By prioritizing self-care, we can ensure that we have the energy and resilience needed to continue our journey of departing from iniquity.

This mindfulness helps to sustain our commitment to following Jesus and to living a life that honors Him.

To depart from iniquity, we must also be willing to seek wisdom and guidance from others. This means being open to learning from the experiences and insights of mature believers. By seeking counsel and mentorship, we can gain valuable support and encouragement in our journey of departing from iniquity. This openness to guidance helps to ensure that we are growing and maturing in our faith, allowing us to depart from iniquity with a wise and discerning heart.

Departing from iniquity requires a commitment to living out our faith in practical ways. This involves demonstrating our commitment to God through our actions, such as showing love, kindness, and compassion to others. By living out our faith, we can make a positive impact and provide a powerful witness to those around us. This practical expression of our faith helps to ensure that our lives reflect the principles of departing from iniquity.

In conclusion, "Depart from iniquity" is a powerful command that emphasizes departure. 2 Timothy 2:19 urges believers to turn away from sinful behaviors and to live lives that reflect their commitment to Christ. Departure involves understanding what iniquity is, cultivating a heart of repentance, being intentional about our actions, seeking the guidance of the Holy Spirit, surrounding ourselves with positive influences, immersing ourselves in God's Word, embracing humility, developing self-discipline, addressing areas of weakness, cultivating gratitude, seeking God's guidance, committing to personal growth, being intentional about relationships, making sacrifices, being patient and persistent, being open to the Holy Spirit, expressing gratitude, investing in others, practicing honesty, seeking justice, prioritizing self-care, seeking wisdom, and living out our faith practically. By embracing this command, we can ensure that our lives reflect our commitment to departing from iniquity and living a life that honors God. In conclusion, "Depart from iniquity" is a command that calls for departure, encouraging us to live a life of righteousness and to turn away from sin, demonstrating our devotion to God through our choices and actions.

Chapter 16 – Desire - "Desire the sincere milk of the word"

1 Peter 2:2 - "As newborn babes, desire the sincere milk of the word, that ye may grow thereby."

This verse emphasizes desire, urging believers to long for the pure and nourishing truths of God's Word, much like a newborn baby craves milk. To desire the sincere milk of the word means to have a deep, earnest longing for the teachings and wisdom found in the Bible. This desire in this context refers to an intense and consistent craving for spiritual growth and nourishment through Scripture. This command encourages us to embrace a lifestyle of learning and growing in our faith by continually seeking the knowledge and understanding that come from God's Word.

Desiring the sincere milk of the word begins with recognizing the importance of the Bible in our lives. Just as a baby relies on milk for sustenance and growth, we rely on God's Word for our spiritual nourishment and development. The Bible provides guidance, encouragement, and wisdom for every aspect of our lives. By understanding the vital role that Scripture plays, we can develop a deep hunger for its teachings. This recognition is the first step in cultivating a genuine desire for God's Word, as it helps us see the necessity of immersing ourselves in the Bible.

To desire the sincere milk of the word, we must prioritize reading and studying the Bible regularly. This means setting aside time each day to engage with Scripture, allowing its truths to penetrate our hearts and minds. By making Bible study a consistent habit, we can ensure that we are continually receiving the spiritual nourishment we need to grow in our faith. This regular engagement with God's Word helps to build a strong foundation for our spiritual lives, allowing us to draw closer to God and to understand His will more clearly. Desiring the sincere milk of the word requires us to approach Scripture with a humble and teachable heart. This means being open to what God wants to teach us and being willing to apply His truths to our lives. By approaching the Bible with humility, we can allow God's Word to transform us and to guide our actions and decisions. This teachability is essential for spiritual growth, as it allows us to be molded and shaped by God's wisdom. As we cultivate a humble and teachable attitude, we can experience the full impact of God's Word in our lives.

To desire the sincere milk of the word, we must also seek to understand the deeper meanings and implications of Scripture. This involves not only reading the Bible but also studying it in depth, using resources such as commentaries, study guides, and discussions with other believers. By delving into the deeper truths of God's Word, we can gain a richer and more comprehensive understanding of His teachings. This deeper study helps to satisfy our spiritual hunger and to equip us with the knowledge we need to live according to God's will. Desiring the sincere milk of the word involves meditating on Scripture and allowing its truths to permeate our hearts and minds. Meditation on God's Word means reflecting on its teachings and considering how they apply to our lives. By taking the time to meditate on Scripture, we can internalize its truths and make them a part of our daily thinking and decision-making processes. This meditation helps to deepen our understanding of God's Word and to strengthen our commitment to living according to its principles.

To desire the sincere milk of the word, we must also be willing to share its truths with others. This means talking about what we are learning from the Bible and encouraging others to seek its wisdom as well. By sharing God's Word with others, we can help to spread its truths and to build a community of believers who are committed to growing in their faith. This sharing also helps to reinforce our own understanding of Scripture and to keep us engaged with its teachings. Desiring the sincere milk of the word requires us to apply its teachings to our lives. This means not only hearing and understanding God's Word but also putting it into practice. By living according to the principles of Scripture, we can demonstrate our commitment to God and to His will. This application of God's Word helps to strengthen our faith and to ensure that its truths are reflected in our actions and decisions. As we strive to live according to God's teachings, we can experience the transformative power of His Word in our lives.

To desire the sincere milk of the word, we must also be persistent in our pursuit of spiritual growth. This means continually seeking to deepen our understanding of God's Word and to grow in our relationship with Him. By being persistent, we can overcome the obstacles and distractions that seek to pull us away from our study of Scripture. This persistence helps to ensure that we are continually nourished by God's Word and that our spiritual growth remains steady and strong. Desiring the sincere milk of the word involves being grateful for the blessings and opportunities that come from studying the Bible. Gratitude helps us to appreciate the value of God's Word and to stay motivated in our pursuit of its truths. By focusing on the goodness and faithfulness of God, we can cultivate a heart of thankfulness that enhances our desire for Scripture. This gratitude helps to keep our hearts aligned with God's will and to remind us of the importance of His Word in our lives.

To desire the sincere milk of the word, we must also seek the guidance and strength of the Holy Spirit. The Holy Spirit provides the wisdom and insight we need to understand and apply God's Word. By relying on the Holy Spirit, we can gain a deeper and more meaningful understanding of Scripture. This dependence on the Holy Spirit helps to ensure that our study of God's Word is fruitful and transformative. As we seek the Spirit's guidance, we can experience the full impact of God's Word in our lives. Desiring the sincere milk of the word requires us to be part of a supportive community of believers. Fellowship with other Christians provides encouragement, accountability, and support in our study of Scripture. By sharing our experiences and insights with others, we can grow together in our understanding of God's Word. This sense of community helps to strengthen our faith and to keep us engaged with Scripture. Being part of a faith community provides a powerful source of encouragement and inspiration, helping us to stay committed to desiring the sincere milk of the word.

To desire the sincere milk of the word, we must also be committed to personal growth and spiritual development. This involves continually seeking to deepen our understanding of God's Word, to grow in our relationship with Him, and to develop our spiritual disciplines. By pursuing spiritual growth, we can strengthen our commitment to desiring the sincere milk of the word and enhance our ability to live according to God's will. This dedication to growth helps to ensure that our faith remains dynamic and alive, continually deepening our connection with God.

Desiring the sincere milk of the word involves being intentional about our actions and decisions. This means making choices that reflect our commitment to God's Word and seeking to live in a way that honors Him. By being intentional, we can ensure that our lives are a reflection of God's love and grace. This intentionality helps to create a positive impact in our communities and to demonstrate our commitment to God's principles. As we make intentional choices that align with God's will, we can desire the sincere milk of the word with a dedicated and focused heart.

To desire the sincere milk of the word, we must also be willing to make sacrifices for the sake of our faith. This means being prepared to give up certain comforts, conveniences, or opportunities that conflict with our commitment to studying God's Word. Sacrifice is a key aspect of desiring the sincere milk of the word, as it demonstrates our willingness to prioritize God's will above our own desires. By making sacrifices, we show that our faith is more important than worldly gain, and we strengthen our resolve to live according to God's principles. As we make sacrifices for our faith, we can desire the sincere milk of the word with a committed and dedicated heart.

Desiring the sincere milk of the word requires us to be patient and persistent in our efforts. Developing a deep and meaningful relationship with God's Word takes time and effort, and it requires us to remain steadfast in our commitment. By being patient and persistent, we can overcome the obstacles and distractions that seek to pull us away from our study of Scripture. This perseverance helps to strengthen our faith and to deepen our relationship with God's Word. As we remain patient and persistent in our pursuit of God's Word, we can desire the sincere milk of the word with a determined and unwavering heart.

To desire the sincere milk of the word, we must also be open to the guidance and direction of the Holy Spirit. The Holy Spirit provides the wisdom and strength we need to navigate life's challenges and to stay focused on our study of Scripture. By being sensitive to the Spirit's leading, we can receive the support and encouragement needed to stay on the path of discipleship. This openness to the Holy Spirit helps to ensure that our relationship with God's Word is continually growing and deepening, allowing us to desire the sincere milk of the word with a true heart.

Desiring the sincere milk of the word requires us to be grateful for the blessings and opportunities that come from studying the Bible. Gratitude helps us to maintain a positive and joyful attitude, even in the face of challenges and difficulties. By focusing on the goodness of God and expressing thankfulness, we can stay motivated and encouraged in our journey of faith. This gratitude helps to keep our hearts centered on God and to remind us of the importance of His Word in our lives. As we cultivate a thankful heart, we can desire the sincere milk of the word with a joyful and appreciative spirit.

To desire the sincere milk of the word, we must also be willing to invest in the well-being of others. This means using our time, resources, and talents to serve and support those around us. By prioritizing the needs of others, we demonstrate the love of Jesus and fulfill His command to love our neighbor as ourselves. This commitment to serving others helps to cultivate a spirit of generosity and compassion, which are essential aspects of desiring the sincere milk of the word. As we invest in the well-being of others, we can desire the sincere milk of the word with a selfless and compassionate heart.

Desiring the sincere milk of the word requires us to be honest and transparent in our relationships. This means being truthful in our words and actions and being willing to admit our mistakes and seek forgiveness. By practicing honesty, we build trust and credibility in our relationships, reflecting the integrity of Jesus. This commitment to truth helps to ensure that our interactions with others are genuine and authentic, allowing us to desire the sincere milk of the word effectively. As we embrace honesty, we can desire the sincere milk of the word with a sincere and truthful heart.

To desire the sincere milk of the word, we must also be willing to seek justice and to stand up for what is right. This means being willing to speak out against injustice and to take action to promote fairness and equality. By prioritizing justice, we demonstrate our commitment to living according to God's values and to making a positive impact in the world. This dedication to justice helps to ensure that our lives reflect the principles of God's kingdom, allowing us to desire the sincere milk of the word with a righteous and just heart.

Desiring the sincere milk of the word involves being mindful of our physical and emotional well-being. Taking care of our bodies and minds by getting enough rest, eating well, and seeking support when needed helps us to better manage the demands of following Jesus. By prioritizing self-care, we can ensure that we have the energy and resilience needed to continue our journey of desiring the sincere milk of the word. This mindfulness helps to sustain our commitment to following Jesus and to living a life that honors Him.

To desire the sincere milk of the word, we must also be willing to seek wisdom and guidance from others. This means being open to learning from the experiences and insights of mature believers. By seeking counsel and mentorship, we can gain valuable support and encouragement in our journey of desiring the sincere milk of the word. This openness to guidance helps to ensure that we are growing and maturing in our faith, allowing us to desire the sincere milk of the word with a wise and discerning heart.

Desiring the sincere milk of the word requires a commitment to living out our faith in practical ways. This involves demonstrating our commitment to God through our actions, such as showing love, kindness, and compassion to others. By living out our faith, we can make a positive impact and provide a powerful witness to those around us. This practical expression of our faith helps to ensure that our lives reflect the principles of desiring the sincere milk of the word.

In conclusion, "Desire the sincere milk of the word" is a powerful command that emphasizes desire. 1 Peter 2:2 urges believers to long for the pure and nourishing truths of God's Word, much like a newborn baby craves milk. Desire involves recognizing the importance of the Bible, prioritizing regular study, approaching Scripture with humility, seeking deeper understanding, meditating on its truths, sharing with others, applying its teachings, being persistent, expressing gratitude, seeking the Holy Spirit's guidance, being part of a supportive community, committing to personal growth, being intentional in our actions, making sacrifices, being patient, being open to guidance, investing in others, practicing honesty, seeking justice, prioritizing self-care, seeking wisdom, and living out our faith practically. By embracing this command, we can ensure that our lives reflect our commitment to desiring the sincere milk of the word and experiencing the fullness of its nourishment and growth. In conclusion, "Desire the sincere milk of the word" is a command that calls for desire, encouraging us to seek the pure and nourishing truths of God's Word and to grow in our faith through its teachings.

Chapter 17 – Deliver - "Deliver the poor and needy"

Psalm 82:4 - "Deliver the poor and needy: rid them out of the hand of the wicked."

This verse emphasizes the action of deliverance, urging believers to actively work to free those who are suffering and oppressed from the grasp of those who exploit and harm them. To deliver the poor and needy means to provide aid, support, and protection to those who are vulnerable and marginalized, ensuring their well-being and safety. This deliverance in this context refers to the deliberate and compassionate effort to intervene on behalf of those in distress, demonstrating God's love and justice through our actions. This command encourages us to embrace a lifestyle of advocacy, generosity, and compassion, committing ourselves to the cause of justice and mercy for those in need.

Delivering the poor and needy begins with recognizing the plight of those who are suffering. It involves opening our eyes and hearts to the realities of poverty, injustice, and oppression that many people face daily. By becoming aware of these issues, we can develop a deep sense of empathy and compassion for those who are struggling. This awareness is the first step in the process of delivering the poor and needy, as it motivates us to take action and to be a voice for the voiceless. Understanding the struggles of others helps us to see the importance of stepping in to help and to make a difference in their lives.

To deliver the poor and needy, we must also be willing to take tangible actions that address their needs. This means providing practical assistance such as food, clothing, shelter, and medical care. By meeting these basic needs, we can offer immediate relief to those who are suffering and help to improve their quality of life. This practical support is essential for delivering the poor and needy, as it provides them with the resources they need to survive and thrive. As we take these tangible actions, we can demonstrate God's love and compassion in meaningful and impactful ways.

Delivering the poor and needy requires us to advocate for systemic change that addresses the root causes of poverty and injustice. This means working to change policies and systems that perpetuate inequality and exploitation. By advocating for fair wages, access to education, healthcare, and other essential services, we can help to create a more just and equitable society. This advocacy is a crucial aspect of delivering the poor and needy, as it seeks to address the underlying issues that contribute to their suffering. As we work for systemic change, we can help to create lasting solutions that benefit those in need.

To deliver the poor and needy, we must also be willing to use our voices to speak out against injustice and to raise awareness about the issues they face. This means educating others about the realities of poverty and oppression and encouraging them to take action as well. By using our voices to advocate for the poor and needy, we can help to amplify their stories and to bring attention to their struggles. This advocacy helps to build a community of support and to mobilize others to join in the effort to deliver those in need. As we speak out against injustice, we can help to create a culture of compassion and action.

Delivering the poor and needy involves building relationships with those we seek to help. This means getting to know their stories, understanding their needs, and offering support in a way that is respectful and empowering. By building genuine relationships, we can offer more effective and meaningful assistance, and we can help to restore dignity and hope to those who are suffering. These relationships are a vital part of delivering the poor and needy, as they allow us to offer personalized support and to walk alongside those in need. As we build these relationships, we can demonstrate God's love and care in a tangible way.

To deliver the poor and needy, we must also be willing to make personal sacrifices. This means giving of our time, resources, and energy to support those who are struggling. By making these sacrifices, we demonstrate our commitment to the well-being of others and our willingness to prioritize their needs above our own. This selflessness is a key aspect of delivering the poor and needy, as it reflects the love and compassion of Jesus. As we make personal sacrifices, we can help to provide the support and care that the poor and needy desperately need.

Delivering the poor and needy requires us to be persistent and resilient in our efforts. Addressing issues of poverty and injustice can be challenging and often requires sustained effort over time. By being persistent, we can continue to make progress and to provide support even when the work is difficult. This resilience helps to ensure that our efforts to deliver the poor and needy are effective and impactful. As we remain committed to this work, we can help to bring about positive change and to improve the lives of those we serve.

To deliver the poor and needy, we must also be committed to prayer and seeking God's guidance in our efforts. Prayer is essential for seeking God's wisdom, strength, and direction as we work to help those in need. By praying for the poor and needy and asking for God's guidance, we can ensure that our actions are aligned with His will and that we are relying on His strength rather than our own. This dependence on God is crucial for delivering the poor and needy, as it helps to sustain and empower our efforts. As we seek God's guidance, we can be confident that He will lead us in the right direction.

Delivering the poor and needy involves being part of a supportive community of believers who share our commitment to this work. Fellowship with other Christians provides encouragement, accountability, and support as we work to help those in need. By joining together with others who are passionate about justice and mercy, we can amplify our efforts and make a greater impact. This sense of community helps to strengthen our resolve and to sustain our efforts over the long term. As we work together with others, we can create a powerful force for good and deliver the poor and needy more effectively.

To deliver the poor and needy, we must also be willing to learn and grow in our understanding of the issues they face. This means educating ourselves about the causes of poverty and injustice and seeking out opportunities for learning and growth. By gaining a deeper understanding of these issues, we can become more effective advocates and supporters for those in need. This commitment to learning helps to ensure that our efforts are informed and impactful. As we seek to grow in our understanding, we can become better equipped to deliver the poor and needy.

Delivering the poor and needy requires us to be creative and innovative in our approach. This means finding new and effective ways to address the needs of those we serve. By thinking outside the box and developing innovative solutions, we can make a greater impact and help to create lasting change. This creativity is essential for delivering the poor and needy, as it allows us to adapt to changing circumstances and to find new opportunities for support and advocacy. As we embrace creativity, we can enhance our efforts and make a meaningful difference in the lives of those in need.

To deliver the poor and needy, we must also be committed to living out our faith in practical ways. This means demonstrating our commitment to God's principles through our actions, such as showing love, kindness, and compassion to others. By living out our faith in practical ways, we can provide a powerful witness to those around us and inspire others to join in our efforts. This practical expression of our faith helps to ensure that our lives reflect the principles of justice and mercy. As we live out our faith, we can help to deliver the poor and needy with a heart full of God's love.

Delivering the poor and needy involves being intentional about our actions and decisions. This means making choices that reflect our commitment to justice and mercy and seeking to live in a way that honors God. By being intentional, we can ensure that our lives are a reflection of God's love and grace. This intentionality helps to create a positive impact in our communities and to demonstrate our commitment to God's principles. As we make intentional choices that align with God's will, we can deliver the poor and needy with a dedicated and focused heart.

To deliver the poor and needy, we must also be willing to confront and challenge systems of oppression and injustice. This means speaking out against policies and practices that harm the vulnerable and advocating for change. By confronting these systems, we can help to create a more just and equitable society. This confrontation is a crucial aspect of delivering the poor and needy, as it seeks to address the root causes of their suffering. As we challenge systems of oppression, we can help to create lasting solutions that benefit those in need.

Delivering the poor and needy requires us to be compassionate and loving in our interactions. This means showing genuine care and concern for others and being willing to help and support them in their journey. By demonstrating compassion, we reflect the love of God and make our efforts more relatable and impactful. This compassion helps to create an environment where people feel valued and open to receiving help. As we show compassion, we can deliver the poor and needy with a heart full of God's love. To deliver the poor and needy, we must also be committed to personal growth and spiritual development. This involves continually seeking to deepen our relationship with God and to grow in our understanding of His Word. By pursuing spiritual growth, we can strengthen our commitment to delivering the poor and needy and enhance our ability to live according to God's will. This dedication to growth helps to ensure that our faith remains dynamic and alive, continually deepening our connection with God.

Delivering the poor and needy involves being part of a supportive community of believers who share our commitment to this work.

Fellowship with other Christians provides encouragement, accountability, and support as we work to help those in need. By joining together with others who are passionate about justice and mercy, we can amplify our efforts and make a greater impact. This sense of community helps to strengthen our resolve and to sustain our efforts over the long term. As we work together with others, we can create a powerful force for good and deliver the poor and needy more effectively.

To deliver the poor and needy, we must also be willing to make sacrifices for the sake of our faith. This means being prepared to give up certain comforts, conveniences,

or opportunities that conflict with our commitment to helping those in need. Sacrifice is a key aspect of delivering the poor and needy, as it demonstrates our willingness to prioritize their needs above our own. By making sacrifices, we show that our faith is more important than worldly gain, and we strengthen our resolve to live according to God's principles. As we make sacrifices for our faith, we can deliver the poor and needy with a committed and dedicated heart.

Delivering the poor and needy requires us to be patient and persistent in our efforts. Addressing issues of poverty and injustice can be challenging and often requires sustained effort over time. By being patient and persistent, we can continue to make progress and to provide support even when the work is difficult. This resilience helps to ensure that our efforts to deliver the poor and needy are effective and impactful. As we remain committed to this work, we can help to bring about positive change and to improve the lives of those we serve.

To deliver the poor and needy, we must also seek God's guidance in all aspects of our efforts. Prayer is essential for seeking God's wisdom, strength, and direction as we work to help those in need. By praying for the poor and needy and asking for God's guidance, we can ensure that our actions are aligned with His will and that we are relying on His strength rather than our own. This dependence on God is crucial for delivering the poor and needy, as it helps to sustain and empower our efforts. As we seek God's guidance, we can be confident that He will lead us in the right direction.

Delivering the poor and needy involves being grateful for the blessings and opportunities that come from helping others. Gratitude helps us to appreciate the value of our efforts and to stay motivated in our pursuit of justice and mercy. By focusing on the goodness and faithfulness of God, we can cultivate a heart of thankfulness that enhances our desire to help those in need. This gratitude helps to keep our hearts aligned with God's will and to remind us of the importance of our work. As we cultivate a thankful heart, we can deliver the poor and needy with a joyful and appreciative spirit.

To deliver the poor and needy, we must also be willing to invest in their well-being. This means using our time, resources, and talents to serve and support those who are struggling. By prioritizing the needs of the poor and needy, we demonstrate the love of Jesus and fulfill His command to love our neighbor as ourselves. This commitment to serving others helps to cultivate a spirit of generosity and compassion, which are essential aspects of delivering the poor and needy. As we invest in the well-being of others, we can deliver the poor and needy with a selfless and compassionate heart.

Delivering the poor and needy requires us to be honest and transparent in our relationships. This means being truthful in our words and actions and being willing to admit our mistakes and seek forgiveness. By practicing honesty, we build trust and credibility in our relationships, reflecting the integrity of Jesus. This commitment to truth helps to ensure that our interactions with others are genuine and authentic, allowing us to deliver the poor and needy effectively. As we embrace honesty, we can deliver the poor and needy with a sincere and truthful heart.

To deliver the poor and needy, we must also be willing to seek justice and to stand up for what is right. This means being willing to speak out against injustice and to take action to promote fairness and equality. By prioritizing justice, we demonstrate our commitment to living according to God's values and to making a positive impact in the world. This dedication to justice helps to ensure that our lives reflect the principles of God's kingdom, allowing us to deliver the poor and needy with a righteous and just heart.

Delivering the poor and needy involves being mindful of our physical and emotional well-being. Taking care of our bodies and minds by getting enough rest, eating well, and seeking support when needed helps us to better manage the demands of following Jesus. By prioritizing self-care, we can ensure that we have the energy and resilience needed to continue our journey of delivering the poor and needy. This mindfulness helps to sustain our commitment to following Jesus and to living a life that honors Him.

To deliver the poor and needy, we must also be willing to seek wisdom and guidance from others. This means being open to learning from the experiences and insights of mature believers. By seeking counsel and mentorship, we can gain valuable support and encouragement in our journey of delivering the poor and needy. This openness to guidance helps to ensure that we are growing and maturing in our faith, allowing us to deliver the poor and needy with a wise and discerning heart.

Delivering the poor and needy requires a commitment to living out our faith in practical ways. This involves demonstrating our commitment to God through our actions, such as showing love, kindness, and compassion to others. By living out our faith, we can make a positive impact and provide a powerful witness to those around us. This practical expression of our faith helps to ensure that our lives reflect the principles of delivering the poor and needy.

In conclusion, "Deliver the poor and needy" is a powerful command that emphasizes deliverance. Psalm 82:4 urges believers to actively work to free those who are suffering and oppressed from the grasp of those who exploit and harm them. Deliverance involves recognizing the plight of those who are suffering, taking tangible actions, advocating for systemic change, using our voices, building relationships, making personal sacrifices, being persistent and resilient, seeking God's guidance, being part of a supportive community, committing to personal growth, being creative, living out our faith practically, being intentional, confronting systems of oppression, showing compassion, expressing gratitude, investing in others, practicing honesty, seeking justice, prioritizing self-care, seeking wisdom, and living out our faith practically. By embracing this command, we can ensure that our lives reflect our commitment to delivering the poor and needy and making a positive impact in the world. In conclusion, "Deliver the poor and needy" is a command that calls for deliverance, encouraging us to actively work to help those in need and to demonstrate God's love and justice through our actions.

Chapter 18 – Dedication - "Do all to the glory of God"

1 Corinthians 10:31 - "Whether therefore ye eat, or drink, or whatsoever ye do, do all to the glory of God."

This verse emphasizes dedication, urging believers to live every aspect of their lives in a way that honors and glorifies God. To do all to the glory of God means to ensure that our actions, words, and thoughts reflect His character and bring praise to Him. This dedication involves a wholehearted commitment to making God's glory the central focus of everything we do. This command encourages us to embrace a lifestyle of continuous worship, where our everyday activities become acts of devotion to God. Doing all to the glory of God begins with understanding that every moment of our lives, no matter how mundane, can be an opportunity to honor Him. This includes daily tasks such as eating, drinking, working, studying, and interacting with others. By approaching these activities with a mindset of dedication to God, we can transform ordinary actions into acts of worship. This perspective helps us to see the significance of our daily lives and to recognize that we can honor God in everything we do. By living with this awareness, we can make our lives a continuous expression of devotion and gratitude to God. To do all to the glory of God, we must cultivate a heart of gratitude. Gratitude helps us to recognize the many blessings and opportunities that God has given us and to respond with thankfulness. By expressing gratitude in all circumstances, we can bring glory to God and demonstrate our appreciation for His goodness and faithfulness. This attitude of gratitude helps to keep our hearts aligned with God's will and to remind us of the importance of honoring Him in everything we do. As we cultivate gratitude, we can make every moment an opportunity to glorify God. Doing all to the glory of God requires us to be intentional about our actions and decisions. This means making choices that reflect our commitment to God's principles and seeking to live in a way that honors Him. By being intentional, we can ensure that our lives are a reflection of God's love and grace. This intentionality helps to create a positive impact in our communities and to demonstrate our dedication to God's glory. As we make intentional choices that align with God's will, we can live lives that bring honor and praise to Him. To do all to the glory of God, we must also be willing to examine our motives. This means considering why we do what we do and ensuring that our actions are driven by a desire to honor God rather than seeking personal gain or recognition. By examining our motives, we can purify our intentions and align them with God's purposes. This self-reflection helps to ensure that our actions are genuine expressions of devotion to God. As we seek to glorify God with pure motives, we can live lives that are pleasing to Him. Doing all to the glory of God involves being humble and recognizing our dependence on Him. This means acknowledging that we cannot navigate life on our own and that we need God's guidance, strength, and provision. By humbling ourselves before God and seeking His help, we open ourselves to His grace and support. This humility allows us to live in a way that honors God and reflects His character. As we depend on God and trust in His goodness, we can experience the peace and security that come from knowing that He is in control. To do all to the glory of God, we must also cultivate a heart of obedience. Obedience means following God's commands and seeking to live according to His principles. By committing to obey God in all aspects of our lives, we can demonstrate our dedication to His glory. This obedience helps to ensure that our actions are aligned with God's will and that we are living in a way that honors Him. As we cultivate a heart of obedience, we can experience the joy and fulfillment that come from living according to God's design. Doing all to the glory of God requires us to be part of a supportive community of believers. Fellowship with other Christians provides encouragement, accountability, and support as we seek to live lives that honor God. By sharing our experiences and challenges with others, we can grow together in our dedication to God's glory. This sense of community helps to strengthen our faith and to keep us focused on our goal of honoring God in everything we do. Being part of a faith community provides a powerful source of encouragement and inspiration, helping us to stay committed to glorifying God. To do all to the glory of God, we must also be committed to personal growth and spiritual development. This involves continually seeking to deepen our understanding of God's Word, to grow in our relationship with Him, and to develop our spiritual disciplines. By pursuing spiritual growth, we can strengthen our commitment to living for God's glory and enhance our ability to reflect His character. This dedication to growth helps to ensure that our faith remains dynamic and alive, continually deepening our connection with God. Doing all to the glory of God involves being mindful of our actions and their impact on others. This means considering how our behavior affects those around us and striving to be a positive influence. By acting with kindness, compassion, and integrity, we can reflect God's love and bring glory to Him. This mindfulness helps to create an environment where people feel valued and respected, and it demonstrates our dedication to living according to God's principles. As we seek to positively impact others, we can glorify God through our relationships and interactions. To do all to the glory of God, we must also be willing to make sacrifices for the sake of our faith. This means being prepared to give up certain comforts, conveniences, or opportunities that conflict with our commitment to honoring God. Sacrifice is a key aspect of doing all to the glory of God, as it demonstrates our willingness to prioritize His will above our own desires. By making sacrifices, we show that our faith is more important than worldly gain, and we strengthen our resolve to live according to God's principles. As we make sacrifices for our faith, we can live lives that bring honor and praise to God. Doing all to the glory of God requires us to be patient and persistent in our efforts.

Living a life that honors God takes time and effort, and it requires us to remain steadfast in our commitment. By being patient and persistent, we can overcome the obstacles and distractions that seek to pull us away from our goal of glorifying God. This perseverance helps to strengthen our faith and to deepen our dedication to God's glory. As we remain patient and persistent in our pursuit of honoring God, we can live lives that are pleasing to Him. To do all to the glory of God, we must also be open to the guidance and direction of the Holy Spirit. The Holy Spirit provides the wisdom and strength we need to navigate life's challenges and to stay focused on our goal of glorifying God. By being sensitive to the Spirit's leading, we can receive the support and encouragement needed to stay on the path of dedication to God's glory. This openness to the Holy Spirit helps to ensure that our relationship with God is continually growing and deepening, allowing us to live lives that bring honor to Him. Doing all to the glory of God requires us to be grateful for the blessings and opportunities that God has given us. Gratitude helps us to maintain a positive and joyful attitude, even in the face of challenges and difficulties. By focusing on the goodness of God and expressing thankfulness, we can stay motivated and encouraged in our journey of faith. This gratitude helps to keep our hearts centered on God and to remind us of the importance of honoring Him in everything we do. As we cultivate a thankful heart, we can live lives that bring glory to God. To do all to the glory of God, we must also be willing to invest in the well-being of others. This means using our time, resources, and talents to serve and support those around us. By prioritizing the needs of others, we demonstrate the love of Jesus and fulfill His command to love our neighbor as ourselves. This commitment to serving others helps to cultivate a spirit of generosity and compassion, which are essential aspects of doing all to the glory of God. As we invest in the well-being of others, we can live lives that bring honor and praise to God. Doing all to the glory of God requires us to be honest and transparent in our relationships. This means being truthful in our words and actions and being willing to admit our mistakes and seek forgiveness. By practicing honesty, we build trust and credibility in our relationships, reflecting the integrity of Jesus. This commitment to truth helps to ensure that our interactions with others are genuine and authentic, allowing us to live lives that bring glory to God. As we embrace honesty, we can live lives that honor God with a sincere and truthful heart. To do all to the glory of God, we must also be willing to seek justice and to stand up for what is right. This means being willing to speak out against injustice and to take action to promote fairness and equality. By prioritizing justice, we demonstrate our commitment to living according to God's values and to making a positive impact in the world. This dedication to justice helps to ensure that our lives reflect the principles of God's kingdom, allowing us to live lives that bring glory to Him. Doing all to the glory of God involves being mindful of our physical and emotional well-being. Taking care of our bodies and minds by getting enough rest, eating well, and seeking support when needed helps us to better manage the demands of following Jesus. By prioritizing self-care, we can ensure that we have the energy and resilience needed to continue our journey of living for God's glory. This mindfulness helps to sustain our commitment to following Jesus and to living a life that honors Him. To do all to the glory of God, we must also be willing to seek wisdom and guidance from others. This means being open to learning from the experiences and insights of mature believers. By seeking counsel and mentorship, we can gain valuable support and encouragement in our journey of living for God's glory. This openness to guidance helps to ensure that we are growing and maturing in our faith, allowing us to live lives that bring honor and praise to God. Doing all

to the glory of God requires a commitment to living out our faith in practical ways. This involves demonstrating our commitment to God through our actions, such as showing love, kindness, and compassion to others. By living out our faith, we can make a positive impact and provide a powerful witness to those around us. This practical expression of our faith helps to ensure that our lives reflect the principles of dedication to God's glory. In conclusion, "Do all to the glory of God" is a powerful command that emphasizes dedication. 1 Corinthians 10:31 urges believers to live every aspect of their lives in a way that honors and glorifies God. Dedication involves understanding that every moment of our lives can be an opportunity to honor God, cultivating a heart of gratitude, being intentional about our actions, examining our motives, practicing humility, cultivating obedience, being part of a supportive community, committing to personal growth, being mindful of our actions' impact, making sacrifices, being patient and persistent, seeking the Holy Spirit's guidance, expressing gratitude, investing in others, practicing honesty, seeking justice, prioritizing self-care, seeking wisdom, and living out our faith practically. By embracing this command, we can ensure that our lives reflect our commitment to doing all to the glory of God and experiencing the fullness of His presence in our lives. In conclusion, "Do all to the glory of God" is a command that calls for dedication, encouraging us to seek to honor and glorify God in everything we do.

Chapter 19 - Diligence - "Diligently keep the commandments of the LORD"

Deuteronomy 6:17 - "Ye shall diligently keep the commandments of the LORD your God, and his testimonies, and his statutes, which he hath commanded thee."

This verse emphasizes diligence, urging believers to be careful, consistent, and thorough in following God's commands. To diligently keep the commandments of the LORD means to commit wholeheartedly to observing God's laws and instructions with great care and perseverance. This diligence involves a steadfast dedication to living according to God's principles and making His will the central focus of our lives. This command encourages us to embrace a lifestyle of constant obedience, where every action, decision, and thought aligns with God's Word.

Diligently keeping the commandments of the LORD begins with understanding the importance of God's laws. The commandments, testimonies, and statutes provided by God are designed to guide us in living righteous and fulfilling lives. They are not merely rules to follow but are expressions of God's love and wisdom meant to protect and bless us. By recognizing the significance of these commandments, we can develop a deep respect and commitment to observing them. This understanding is the first step in cultivating a diligent heart that seeks to honor God in all things.

To diligently keep the commandments of the LORD, we must prioritize studying and knowing God's Word. This means setting aside regular time to read, meditate on, and learn from the Bible. By immersing ourselves in Scripture, we can understand God's will more clearly and discover how to apply His teachings to our daily lives. This regular engagement with God's Word helps to build a strong foundation for our faith and ensures that we are equipped to live according to His commandments. As we study the Bible diligently, we can grow in wisdom and knowledge, making it easier to follow God's instructions faithfully.

Diligently keeping the commandments of the LORD requires us to be intentional about our actions and decisions. This means making choices that reflect our commitment to God's principles and avoiding actions that contradict His will. By being intentional, we can ensure that our lives are a reflection of God's love, grace, and righteousness. This intentionality helps to create a positive impact in our communities and demonstrates our dedication to God's commandments. As we make deliberate choices that align with God's Word, we can live lives that honor Him and bring glory to His name.

To diligently keep the commandments of the LORD, we must also cultivate a heart of obedience. Obedience means following God's commands even when it is difficult or inconvenient. It requires us to trust in God's wisdom and to submit to His authority in all areas of our lives. By committing to obey God in every aspect, we demonstrate our faithfulness and dedication to His will. This obedience helps to ensure that our actions are aligned with God's principles and that we are living in a way that pleases Him. As we cultivate a heart of obedience, we can experience the blessings and joy that come from living according to God's design.

Diligently keeping the commandments of the LORD involves being humble and recognizing our dependence on Him. This means acknowledging that we cannot live righteously on our own and that we need God's guidance, strength, and provision. By humbling ourselves before God and seeking His help, we open ourselves to His grace and support. This humility allows us to live in a way that honors God and reflects His character. As we depend on God and trust in His goodness, we can experience the peace and security that come from knowing that He is in control.

To diligently keep the commandments of the LORD, we must also be vigilant in guarding our hearts and minds against influences that lead us away from God. This means being mindful of the media we consume, the company we keep, and the activities we engage in. By protecting ourselves from negative influences, we can stay focused on God's Word and avoid temptations that could lead us astray. This vigilance is essential for maintaining a diligent heart that seeks to honor God in all things. As we guard our hearts and minds, we can stay committed to following God's commandments faithfully.

Diligently keeping the commandments of the LORD requires us to be part of a supportive community of believers. Fellowship with other Christians provides encouragement, accountability, and support as we seek to live lives that honor God. By sharing our experiences and challenges with others, we can grow together in our dedication to God's commandments. This sense of community helps to strengthen our faith and to keep us focused on our goal of living according to God's will. Being part of a faith community provides a powerful source of encouragement and inspiration, helping us to stay committed to diligently keeping God's commandments.

To diligently keep the commandments of the LORD, we must also be committed to personal growth and spiritual development. This involves continually seeking to deepen our understanding of God's Word, to grow in our relationship with Him, and to develop our spiritual disciplines. By pursuing spiritual growth, we can strengthen our commitment to living according to God's commandments and enhance our ability to reflect His character. This dedication to growth helps to ensure that our faith remains dynamic and alive, continually deepening our connection with God.

Diligently keeping the commandments of the LORD involves being mindful of our actions and their impact on others. This means considering how our behavior affects those around us and striving to be a positive influence. By acting with kindness, compassion, and integrity, we can reflect God's love and bring glory to Him. This mindfulness helps to create an environment where people feel valued and respected, and it demonstrates our dedication to living according to God's principles. As we seek to positively impact others, we can honor God through our relationships and interactions.

To diligently keep the commandments of the LORD, we must also be willing to make sacrifices for the sake of our faith. This means being prepared to give up certain comforts, conveniences, or opportunities that conflict with our commitment to following God's commandments. Sacrifice is a key aspect of diligently keeping God's commandments, as it demonstrates our willingness to prioritize His will above our own desires. By making sacrifices, we show that our faith is more important than worldly gain, and we strengthen our resolve to live according to God's principles. As we make sacrifices for our faith, we can live lives that honor and glorify God.

Diligently keeping the commandments of the LORD requires us to be patient and persistent in our efforts. Living a life that honors God takes time and effort, and it requires us to remain steadfast in our commitment. By being patient and persistent, we can overcome the obstacles and distractions that seek to pull us away from our goal of diligently keeping God's commandments. This perseverance helps to strengthen our faith and to deepen our dedication to God's will. As we remain patient and persistent in our pursuit of honoring God, we can live lives that are pleasing to Him.

To diligently keep the commandments of the LORD, we must also be open to the guidance and direction of the Holy Spirit. The Holy Spirit provides the wisdom and strength we need to navigate life's challenges and to stay focused on our goal of diligently keeping God's commandments. By being sensitive to the Spirit's leading, we can receive the support and encouragement needed to stay on the path of dedication to God's will. This openness to the Holy Spirit helps to ensure that our relationship with God is continually growing and deepening, allowing us to live lives that bring honor to Him.

Diligently keeping the commandments of the LORD requires us to be grateful for the blessings and opportunities that God has given us. Gratitude helps us to maintain a positive and joyful attitude, even in the face of challenges and difficulties. By focusing on the goodness of God and expressing thankfulness, we can stay motivated and encouraged in our journey of faith. This gratitude helps to keep our hearts centered on God and to remind us of the importance of diligently keeping His commandments in everything we do. As we cultivate a thankful heart, we can live lives that bring glory to God.

To diligently keep the commandments of the LORD, we must also be willing to invest in the well-being of others. This means using our time, resources, and talents to serve and support those around us. By prioritizing the needs of others, we demonstrate the love of Jesus and fulfill His command to love our neighbor as ourselves. This commitment to serving others helps to cultivate a spirit of generosity and compassion, which are essential aspects of diligently keeping God's commandments. As we invest in the well-being of others, we can live lives that bring honor and praise to God.

Diligently keeping the commandments of the LORD requires us to be honest and transparent in our relationships. This means being truthful in our words and actions and being willing to admit our mistakes and seek forgiveness. By practicing honesty, we build trust and credibility in our relationships, reflecting the integrity of Jesus. This commitment to truth helps to ensure that our interactions with others are genuine and authentic, allowing us to live lives that bring glory to God. As we embrace honesty, we can live lives that honor God with a sincere and truthful heart.

To diligently keep the commandments of the LORD, we must also be willing to seek justice and to stand up for what is right. This means being willing to speak out against injustice and to take action to promote fairness and equality. By prioritizing justice, we demonstrate our commitment to living according to God's values and to making a positive impact in the world. This dedication to justice helps to ensure that our lives reflect the principles of God's kingdom, allowing us to live lives that bring glory to Him.

Diligently keeping the commandments of the LORD involves being mindful of our physical and emotional well-being. Taking care of our bodies and minds by getting enough rest, eating well, and seeking support when needed helps us to better manage the demands of following Jesus. By prioritizing self-care, we can ensure that we have the energy and resilience needed to continue our journey of diligently keeping God's commandments. This mindfulness helps to sustain our commitment to following Jesus and to living a life that honors Him.

To diligently keep the commandments of the LORD, we must also be willing to seek wisdom and guidance from others. This means being open to learning from the experiences and insights of mature believers. By seeking counsel and mentorship, we can gain valuable support and encouragement in

our journey of diligently keeping God's commandments. This openness to guidance helps to ensure that we are growing and maturing in our faith, allowing us to live lives that bring honor and praise to God.

Diligently keeping the commandments of the LORD requires a commitment to living out our faith in practical ways. This involves demonstrating our commitment to God through our actions, such as showing love, kindness, and compassion to others. By living out our faith, we can make a positive impact and provide a powerful witness to those around us. This practical expression of our faith helps to ensure that our lives reflect the principles of diligence in keeping God's commandments.

In conclusion, "Diligently keep the commandments of the LORD" is a powerful command that emphasizes diligence. Deuteronomy 6:17 urges believers to be careful, consistent, and thorough in following

God's commands. Diligence involves understanding the importance of God's laws, prioritizing regular study of His Word, being intentional about our actions, cultivating a heart of obedience, practicing humility, guarding our hearts and minds, being part of a supportive community, committing to personal growth, being mindful of our actions' impact, making sacrifices, being patient and persistent, seeking the Holy Spirit's guidance, expressing gratitude, investing in others, practicing honesty, seeking justice, prioritizing self-care, seeking wisdom, and living out our faith practically. By embracing this command, we can ensure that our lives reflect our commitment to diligently keeping God's commandments and experiencing the fullness of His blessings. In conclusion, "Diligently keep the commandments of the LORD" is a command that calls for diligence, encouraging us to live according to God's principles and to honor Him in everything we do.

Conclusion

As we reach the conclusion of "Scriptural Commands for Modern Times- Living God's Word Today Volume 2," it's clear that the commands of Scripture are not just historical instructions but living words that are incredibly relevant to our lives today. Throughout this book, we've explored how these commands can guide us in every aspect of our lives, from how we interact with others to how we make decisions and handle the pressures of the modern world. The teachings we've examined are more than just rules to follow—they are a blueprint for living a life that is fulfilling, purposeful, and aligned with God's will. This journey has shown us that when we live according to God's commands, we open ourselves up to a life of peace, joy, and deep spiritual satisfaction. These commands help us navigate the complexities of today's world with wisdom and grace, offering us a steady foundation in a time when everything else seems uncertain. As you close this book, remember that the lessons learned here are meant to be carried forward into your daily life. The truths of Scripture are not just for the pages of a book; they are for the everyday moments, the tough decisions, and the interactions with the people around you. Let these commands continue to guide you, shape you, and draw you closer to God as you go about your life. The journey doesn't end here; in fact, it's only just beginning. By applying what you've learned, you will continue to grow in your faith, deepen your relationship with God, and experience the life He has planned for you—a life that is rich with meaning, filled with His love, and grounded in His truth. So take these commands to heart, live them out each day, and watch as God's Word transforms your life and the lives of those around you. As you go forward, may you always remember that God's commands are not just ancient words but living instructions for today, designed to lead you into the abundant life that God has promised. Let His Word be your guide, your comfort, and your strength as you continue to walk in His

ways, living out His truth in a world that desperately needs the light
and hope that only He can provide.

Don't miss out!

Visit the website below and you can sign up to receive emails whenever Joshua Rhoades publishes a new book. There's no charge and no obligation.

https://books2read.com/r/B-A-AJLBB-BGAZE

BOOKS 2 READ

Connecting independent readers to independent writers.

Did you love *Scriptural Commands for Modern Times Living God's Word Today Volume 2*? Then you should read *The Shout That Stopped The Saviour*[1] by Joshua Rhoades!

[2]

"The Shout That Stopped The Saviour" explores the remarkable story of Blind Bartimaeus, whose faith and desperation moved Jesus to perform one of the most memorable miracles in the Gospels. Mark 10:46-52 tells of a blind beggar whose cry for mercy halted Jesus on His journey, leading to a life-changing encounter. Bartimaeus' story goes beyond a physical healing; it illustrates the power of persistent faith, the importance of boldness in adversity, and the deep compassion Jesus has for those who seek Him earnestly.

In Jericho, Bartimaeus sat by the roadside, marginalized and overlooked, with only a desperate plea to offer. When he heard that Jesus of Nazareth was passing by, he didn't hesitate. Despite the crowd's attempts to silence him, Bartimaeus cried out louder, "Jesus, thou Son

---

1. https://books2read.com/u/b5DdNk

2. https://books2read.com/u/b5DdNk

of David, have mercy on me!" This was no ordinary shout—it was a cry from the depths of his soul, recognizing Jesus as the Messiah and pleading for mercy from the only One who could truly change his circumstances.

Bartimaeus' unwavering faith and determination in the face of opposition stand out. He wasn't discouraged by his status or blindness but saw with the eyes of faith what others could not—that Jesus had the power to heal and transform his life. His shout was an act of faith that stopped Jesus in His tracks.

"The Shout That Stopped The Saviour" invites readers to reflect on their own cries for help and expressions of faith in desperation. Bartimaeus' story challenges us to consider whether we, too, are willing to cry out to Jesus with boldness and persistence. It reminds us that Jesus hears the sincere cries of those who seek Him and responds with compassion and power, offering an invitation to experience the same transformative faith in our own lives.